D1759786

01603 773114
email: tis@ccn.ac.uk   @CCN_Library   /ccninformationstore
ccnlibraryblog.wordpress.com

21 DAY LOAN ITEM
NORFOLK HOUSE

Please return <u>on or before</u> the last date stamped above

A fine will be charged for overdue items

CITY
COLLEGE
NORWICH

216 737

The Impact and Evaluation of Major Sporting Events

Ever more cities and countries are bidding to stage major sporting events. One of the main reasons for this is the economic benefit expected by decision makers and citizens. However, events such as the Olympic Games, the super bowl or the FIFA football world cup are so complex that the aims of the various stakeholders are often incompatible. Therefore the key welfare issue is whether or not major sporting events really achieve efficient outcomes and justify investments of scarce public resources.

The aim of politicians is to attract new investment to their city or region in order to develop infrastructure such as telecommunications, transportation, housing or even sport and entertainment facilities. Sporting events are also intended to achieve intangible ends such as a better image, more know-how, stronger networks, emotional commitment and additional cultural benefits and enhanced identity. All these so called 'event structures' can improve sites in a city/region by strengthening certain location factors. They may improve general living conditions in the longer term and also boost the income of citizens by attracting new businesses, tourists, conventions or new events. Finally they may foster economic growth at the city, regional or national level.

The Impact and Evaluation of Major Sporting Events is of particular interest for anyone who intends to enter a bidding process for a major sporting event. It offers the host of an event a good introduction to the potential ways to generate economic benefits and will enhance understanding of the economics behind major sporting events.

This book was previously published as a special issue of *European Sport Management Quarterly*.

Holger Preuss is professor for Sport Economy and Sport Management at the Johannes Gutenberg-University in Mainz, Germany. He is visiting professor at the Beijing Sport University in order to support Olympic research.

The Impact and Evaluation of Major Sporting Events

Edited by
Holger Preuss

NORWICH CITY COLLEGE LIBRARY		
Stock No.	216737	
Class	338. 4791 PRE	
Cat.		Proc.	3wr

Routledge
Taylor & Francis Group
LONDON AND NEW YORK

First published 2007 by Routledge
2 Park Square, Milton Park, Abingdon, Oxon, OX14 4RN

Simultaneously published in the USA and Canada
by Routledge
270 Madison Ave, New York, NY 10016

Routledge is an imprint of the Taylor & Francis Group, an informa business

© 2007 Edited by Holger Preuss

Typeset by Datapage International Ltd., Dublin, Ireland
Printed and bound in Great Britain by MPG, Bodmin, Cornwall

All rights reserved. No part of this book may be reprinted or reproduced or utilised
in any form or by any electronic, mechanical, or other means, now known or
hereafter invented, including photocopying and recording, or in any information
storage or retrieval system, without permission in writing from the publishers.

British Library Cataloguing in Publication Data
A catalogue record for this book is available from the British Library

Library of Congress Cataloging in Publication Data

ISBN 10: 0-415-44924-3
ISBN 13: 978-0-415-44924-3 hbk

Contents

Impact and Evaluation of Major Sporting Events

HOLGER PREUSS

Johannes Gutenberg-University in Mainz, Germany

Ever more cities and countries are bidding to stage major sporting events. One of the main reasons for this is the economic benefit expected by decision makers and citizens. From the perspective of economics, the key welfare issue is whether or not major sporting events really achieve efficient outcomes given the potentially incompatible aims of different stakeholders which invariably lead to some debatable investments of scarce public resources.

A key aim of politicians is to attract new investment to their city or region in order to develop infrastructure such as telecommunication, transportation, housing or even sport and entertainment facilities. Sporting events are also intended to achieve intangible ends such as a better image, more know-how, stronger networks, emotional commitment and additional cultural benefits and enhanced identity (see Figure 1). All these 'event structures' can improve sites in a city/region by strengthening certain location factors. Those may improve general living conditions in the longer term but also boost the income of citizens by attracting new businesses, tourists, conventions or new events. These finally may foster economic growth at the city, regional or national level.

This issue intends to contribute to the (rather uncertain) expectations of politicians and citizens. Two contributions analyse input factors (change of physical infrastructure and human resources) which may have improved location factors for the respective hosts. Two others focus on the measurable economic output of events, and one contribution seeks to explain the political circumstances for investment of scarce public resources to attract major sporting events.

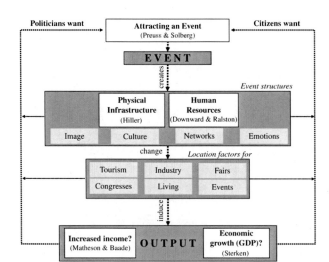

Figure 1. Economic output of major sporting events and contributions to this issue

However, major sporting events are not a panacea, and some scientific controversy has developed over whether major sporting events have a measurable and lasting economic effect for a city, region or nation. This collection of articles intends to untangle some of the arguments relating to the economic consequences of staging major sporting events.

A very important distinction has to be made between the measurement of the output of event-related activities and event-related changes of production factors which may induce future non-event-related economic activity. This issue contains two articles (Hiller and Downward & Ralston) that deal with the latter. The Canadian urban sociologist Harry Hiller focuses on the Olympics and the post-Games urban transformations. The British sport economists Paul M. Downward and Rita Ralston identify how the experience of volunteering at a major sporting event affects interest, participation and subsequent volunteering in sport, and also volunteering in non-sport contexts. Both articles are based on case studies and can certainly only reflect what happened at the specific events to which they relate and illustrate one of several other production factors affected by major sporting events.

Most often, economic studies of major sporting events analyse the event-output and are based on circle theory. The models use the expenditure approach by considering all direct and indirect spending linked with an event and its consequential induced effects. However, there are two shortcomings to be mentioned: studies do not consider effects resulting from a long-lasting change in location factors and analysts cannot isolate all event effects from other activities of the event host city/region which also contribute to economic activity. Despite these problems this issue offers two important contributions using sophisticated models aimed at detecting changes in economic indicators caused by major sporting events. Victor A. Matheson and Robert A. Baade display evidence from host cities (1970–2001) indicating that although the Super Bowl contributes additional income for the host community, it only generates approximately one-quarter of what the boosters have promised to the cities. The Dutch economist Elmer Sterken uses an even broader approach presenting *ex-post* cross-national-event results for the Summer Olympic Games and the FIFA World Cup. He is able to show that the intensive investments into infrastructure in the years prior to the Olympic Games have at least induced economic growth.

However, there are several factors that make it difficult to evaluate the economic efficiency of major sporting events and this makes it difficult either to use case studies as benchmarks for other locations, or to use broad economic indicators (in a limited time frame) to make general judgements about the potential for the economic success of events.

Major sporting events vary considerably in terms of required financial inputs and the possible long-term outputs. Furthermore, there are not enough major sporting events in one period, say the past 15 years, to derive compelling statistical evidence. This selection of articles can only focus on single factors and on different types of events, although with considerable variety. These include:

1. *Single versus multi-sport events:* this issue covers different major sporting events. The Olympic Games (summer and winter editions) and the Commonwealth Games represent multi-sport events while the FIFA football World Cups and Super Bowls are single-sport events.
2. *Location of the event:* articles incorporated focus on events in particular locations (Calgary and Manchester) as well as on several events irrespective of their location (Super Bowls, Olympic Games and FIFA World Cups).
3. *Region affected by the event:* finally, the issue contains articles focusing on events circulating around the world (Olympics, FIFA World Cups and Commonwealth Games) and others circulating in one country (Super Bowls). The events either affect a city and region (Olympics, Commonwealth Games and Super Bowls) or the whole nation (FIFA Football World Cups).

This differentiation of events underlines already how difficult it is to measure the economic efficiency of staging an event. This is compounded by the varying levels and quality of infrastructure, differing goals and complexity of structural changes within a city or region. Furthermore the lengthy time frame from preparation to staging and the evolution of benefits from changed location factors complicate measurement.

The discussion of whether to invest or not in major sporting events is often reduced to the analyses of the measurable economic output of an event. The selection of articles in this issue, therefore, also incorporates both contributions analysing changes of 'event structures' and contributions which provide models to analyse economic growth. The final article (Preuss & Solberg) seeks to explain the desire of politicians and citizens to stage a major sporting event. The authors look to find evidence of why, on the one hand, the number of bid cities for major sporting events is increasing while, on the other hand, more and more sport economists doubt the net economic benefit of staging such events. Based on the 'want' of citizens who expect various (economic) benefits, politicians are often pressed to at least consider bidding for an event. However, market failure due to public goods and positive externalities produced by an event militate against the level of investment of private resources necessary to win a bid in today's bidding competitions. Therefore, winning the right to stage an event requires at least partial finance from public resources. Whether this is good for a city and for public welfare has to be analysed individually from bid city to bid city.

This issue can only highlight some of the factors that will enhance understanding of the economics behind major sporting events. While it offers a good introduction of various aspects of the potential to generate economic benefits for the host of an event, I would underline for readers the need not to deduce inductive evidence for specific event applications from both case studies and average results on economic growth.

Holger Preuss

Post-event Outcomes and the Post-modern Turn: The Olympics and Urban Transformations

HARRY H. HILLER

University of Calgary, Alberta, Canada

There is considerable agreement that the Olympics is not just about sport but is also about politics (Espy, 1979; Andranovich *et al.*, 2001) and capitalist economics (Lenskyj, 2000). It was not until recently that it has become increasingly clear that the Olympics are also about cities (Essex & Chalkley, 1998; Hiller, 1999). The primary signal of this fact comes from city leaders themselves that do not think of the Olympics just as sport but as an opportunity to accomplish items on their own urban agenda. The question of why cities are willing to mobilize resources and energy to even become a candidate city, let alone be willing to serve as a host city, defies simple explanations but implies the existence of important urban objectives.

Even though the primary purpose of being a host city is to serve as the location for sporting events, there must be much more at stake than merely providing a venue for sport competitions. Much attention has been given to the economic impact and tourism impact of hosting the Olympics which stresses the role of the Games themselves. What has been neglected is how the Olympics are related to the long-term goals of the city. The Olympics must be understood not only in terms of the preparation and hosting phase but also in terms of the post-event consequences to complete what is known as the Olympic cycle (the four phases being the bid phase, the preparation phase, the event phase and the post-event phase (Hiller, 1998)). The most concrete long-term impact is related to the built environment. In fact, one of the unique aspects of the Olympics as a mega-event is that while it is both a short-term and high profile event, hosting the Olympics almost always involves significant capital costs through the construction of specialized buildings and other infrastructural improvements. Thus, if there is any long-term impact on cities, it is usually related to these capital expenditures and the built environment changes that result. It is not just the structures created for the Olympics itself but the side effects, residual effects, or parallel linkages (Hiller, 1998) that play a role in transforming the urban environment that is important. Cities often use the Olympics to accomplish other objectives that may support the Games but which are of even greater long-term value. Another issue is that of the after-use of Olympic facilities and infrastructure whose size and scale may not always be consonant with future urban needs. The 110,000 seat stadium built to accommodate the Olympics in Sydney is one example of a structure that was built with far too much capacity for after-use (Cashman, 2006), and velodromes are another example of a structure with little continuing demand. Given the expense involved, after-use is a major issue, and cities often have difficulty aligning Olympic needs with post-event usage in the light of capital cost expenditures.

From the point of view of understanding the long-term impact of the Olympics on cities, the construction of event facilities are perhaps the most enduring and visible legacy. Infrastructural improvements such as in transportation or urban renewal may have been some of the key benefits anticipated by a host city in winning the bid. But some Olympic facilities may have little utility in the post-Olympic period. What role do they play in cities and how does their post-Olympic usage reflect what is happening to the urban order? In other words, how does the Olympic agenda impact the built environment of cities on a long-term basis, and how are these structures adapted for long-term usage? Above all, how are they related to the changing nature and structure of contemporary city life? These questions are not asked from the perspectives of architecture, engineering, or economics but from an urban perspective in terms of how post-event usage relates to urban processes. They are also asked in a sociological context in which usage is understood as human behaviour.

The focus of this paper will primarily be on specialized event structures. In many ways, they are lasting Olympic legacies in the city but they also represent dilemmas and challenges for cities. The issue of after-use will be related to how the contemporary Olympics are connected to urban transformations, for the shape and form of the modern Olympics both contribute to and reflect the transformations of the urban order that is occurring. Once the Olympics have been placed in this urban context, the long-term impact of the Olympics on cities can be understood. In comparison to the Summer Olympics, the Winter Olympics provide a different illustration of this process, and sufficient time has now passed to support an analysis of the 1988 Calgary Winter Olympics. Some additional references will be made to the 2002 Salt Lake City Winter Olympics.

The Olympics and the Restructuring of Cities

Much has been written about how the urban order is undergoing a massive transformation (Soja, 2001). Five characteristics of this urban restructuring can be identified, and then the after-use of Olympic facilities can be related to the post-modern shift in urban transformation.

Cities and the Globalization of Capital, Culture and Information Flows

The globalization of the economy has meant that cities are now part of a hierarchy of urban places in which power flows from global cities which serve as command centres and peripheral cities struggle for a significant place within the global urban hierarchy. Of particular importance is the emergence of what has been called the "entrepreneurial city" in which coalitions of urban elites unite to promote the economic development of their city (Harvey, 1988; Hall & Hubbard, 1998). Elite coalitions involve politicians, planners, real estate developers and business leaders attempting to make their cities more competitive by attracting new sources of funding and direct investment to support various forms of business development and employment creation, as well as to improve the built environment either for its own sake or to change the image of a city. Globalization therefore means greater intercity competition, both nationally and internationally, in which entrepreneurial cities seek a competitive edge.

The role that the Olympics play in place marketing is well known but usually is acknowledged more indirectly (Whitson & MacIntosh, 1996; Roche, 2000). The emphasis in presentations to the International Olympic Committee (IOC) is usually on the city's technical competencies to host the Olympics whereas the rationales presented to local and national constituencies emphasizes spinoff effects such as employment creation (often not explicitly acknowledged as short term), tax revenues and tourism development. But lurking not far behind these economic justifications is the global publicity given to the host city that usually results in a concerted public relations effort to market and massage the image of the city throughout the various phases of the Olympic cycle. Urban elite coalitions visualize the Olympics as an opportunity to enhance and broaden the profile of the city not just for its "demonstration effects" (i.e. to demonstrate that the city has the capacity or ability to host such an event) but to "showcase" the city as an attractive place for investment. In some cases, this is public investment for infrastructural change from higher levels of government (which will be discussed below), but a central goal is also to make the city attractive as a place for private investment, including from international sources (Searle, 2003, p. 125). Cities bidding from developing countries or countries wishing to redefine their global position have been especially attracted to the Olympics for this reason. The Olympics then becomes a tool in the more general goal of greater economic development as represented by urban boosterism (Smyth, 1994). This role of the Olympics has become particularly important in a global economy characterized by more competition between cities. Presumably, then, the ability to mobilize capital for Olympic infrastructure is considered to be symbolic of a city's capacity to compete with other cities by taking on such a large-scale multi-faceted project. But it is not just the Olympic facilities themselves that are important but the supporting infrastructure of transportation, housing and leisure activities that must be upgraded (discussed below) in order to enhance the city's environment and its global appeal.

The Economic Restructuring of Cities

One of the primary characteristics of cities in the developed world has been the shift to a post-Fordist economy. This is the process of deindustrialization where factory-type jobs and a manufacturing producer economy have been replaced by information technologies and a service economy. Business services, finance, and leisure industries take on a much more prominent role, and heavy industry almost disappears to developing countries where labour is less costly.

There are two consequences of this development for the importance of the Olympics for cities. One is that post-industrial cities are eager to either find uses for old buildings that once had an industrial use, or they are interested in replacing them with buildings that are more relevant to the service economy. It is in this context that the Olympics become a useful tool in the process of urban regeneration. The transformation of waterfront or inner city locations (e.g. Barcelona: Moragas and Botella, 1995), whose value was once important for industrial uses, serve as a typical example of how cities conceive of the Olympics as a prompter to some sort of transformation of the built environment. Almost every city that engages in the construction of significant new buildings for the Olympics targets older areas requiring some kind of renewal (Gratton & Henry, 2001).

The second aspect of this economic restructuring is that the shift to a service economy results in a different labour pool within the city. A service economy means a post-industrial city that supports leisure industries which are vital to a successful Olympics, and this point will be discussed further later. It also means a city with the urban ambience (including cleaner air) that Olympic administrators and athletes value. Service workers (primarily white-collar employees) fit the model of personnel required as volunteers for the Olympic effort. Persons with office jobs are more likely to be available and interested in volunteering and fit the profile of conscientious, disciplined and image-conscious workers which the Olympics require. Such people are also more likely to afford tickets to

Olympic events. In short, the Olympics fit well with an urban service-based economy.

In both developed and less developed cities, the Olympics provide the occasion for cities to appeal to the public sector (particularly the national government) for the allocation of funds not otherwise available. It legitimates public expenditures in one city that may not be available to other cities in the same country. The IOC likes to think of the Olympics' lasting contribution to a host city as a "legacy" that is almost always conceived of as a sporting legacy. But cities are increasingly interested in a legacy beyond the sporting world and that contributes to making the city a better place. In that regard, preparation for the Olympics, especially in recent years, has stimulated investment forums that are oriented towards using the Olympics to encourage inward investment or for local businesses to seize the occasion of the Olympics to develop new business opportunities. Private businesses, particularly in the tourism industry, may become involved in new construction or renovations and, in general, the Olympics often serve as a catalyst in the beautification, restoration or refurbishing of varying aspects of the built environment. For example, one month before the Olympics in Athens, it seemed that everywhere everything was under construction or renovation (whether directly Olympic related or not) in preparation for the Olympics, which served as a completion goal for all kinds of actions (e.g. painting, cleaning, modernizing) that otherwise might have been completed without a uniform time-line.

There is also the likelihood that Olympic sites themselves can have a spillover effect on adjacent property that spurs new development. Olympic venues often lead to vastly improved public spaces that also usually make adjacent property more valuable and desirable which attracts a more upscale class of residents and therefore more upscale uses. Olympic related housing (athletes, media, etc.) in particular must be built to standards for their occupants and also are often built under pressure to be sold at high market values to pay for the construction costs (and perhaps even to make a profit). After-use, then, might shift to persons of higher income rather than the provision of housing for low-income persons. Barcelona, for example, experienced this kind of gentrification as the Olympic Village (Icaria) eventually transformed the area from a working class district to a community largely inhabited by upper-middle and upper-class residents after the Games (Kennett & de Moragas, 2006). This raises the question about who in a city benefits the most from hosting the Olympics, and it is for this reason that the Games almost always trigger opposition by those who prefer that a city's scarce resources be directed to benefit those most disadvantaged rather than supporting profit-making and the embourgeoisment of the city. Since one of the primary characteristics of the post-modern city is the increasing polarization of urban populations in which the wealthy and the poor have very different urban lives, the Olympics then are often viewed as reinforcing this trend in the post-Fordist city. Thus, the Olympics can impact the built environment of cities in a variety of ways.

In short, the Olympics can serve a useful role for a city engaged in some type of restructuring or renovation. It facilitates the process of reconditioning and usually leads to the construction of new facilities that contributes to a changing built environment. These changes usually occur in support of a shift by the city to an urban service economy but with differential effects on the city's residents. It is also possible that beautification efforts might mask growing inequalities in a restructured city.

Leisure Consumption and the City

If the city was once the place for the space intensive and labour intensive activity of the factory and then the office, the post-modern city with its emphasis on services is now increasingly coming to be defined by consumptive leisure in culture, dining and entertainment (Clark, 2004). Cultural districts and museums, branded retail emporiums, themed restaurants and bars, mega theatre complexes, virtual arcades, sport venues, hotels, and other leisure areas have become high profile "landscapes of consumption" in what Zukin (1995) has called the "symbolic economy". Using Disney-esque surreal design, the end result has been "sim cities" or "fantasy cities" in which unique architecture is used not as works of art but as a mechanism to foster spending and entertainment, whether by tourists or urban residents, and to create images whether real or imagined (Hannigan, 1998).

The Olympics, of course, are an entertainment spectacle par excellence. But, more importantly, it also reinforces the direction of this trend towards consumptive leisure because hosting the Olympics requires preparation for high-demand consumer behaviour. From the point of view of visitors as well as local residents, the Olympics intensify leisure consumption and, as will be shown, become intimately related to facility after-use. It is not surprising, then, that the consumption industries are major supporters of the Olympics because they benefit through all stages of the Olympic cycle. Industry members even use the Olympic cycle to enhance their product through things such as the building or redevelopment of hotels, tourism packages for visitors and the opening of new leisure activities (Preuss, 2004). Indeed, from the urban merchant's point of view, and from the point of view of governments who receive retail taxes, one of the major objectives of the Olympics is to increase revenues through consumer spending. From the point of view of this analysis, what is important is that the Olympics both contribute to and reinforce this trend towards leisure consumption in the post-modern city.

The Polycentric Mega-city

Whereas cities have always had a strong central core, the continuing growth of cities to produce mega-cities has meant that cities have now become more de-centered into vast urban regions. The regionalization of cities has created metropolitan areas consisting of a plurality of urban municipalities. The mega-city then is not just one city but a multiple of cities forming an urban region. There are two implications of this trend for the Olympics.

First, the range of facilities that is needed for Olympic events usually means a dispersal of those facilities within an urban region. While the IOC and athletes might prefer a compact Olympics in which all venues are in the same general vicinity, that is not possible, and the increasing size of cities makes transportation between sites a major issue. The dispersal of competition and practice sites (often amidst heavy traffic) and even the choice of location of athletes' villages (sometimes in more than one location) mean that the modern Olympics cannot be contained within a single urban space, and its activities are distributed throughout the metropolitan galaxy.

The second point of some significance is that the modern Olympics with the various constituents of the "Olympic family", from athletes, federations and sponsoring corporations as well as support services and media requirements, has meant that the Olympics can only be held in large cities with a strong regionalized support structure. For example, central city hotels are not usually adequate and hotels in the urban region are required. Cities must be large enough to support a variety of international air carriers in order to service Olympic needs properly. Hosting the summer Olympics is increasingly limited to only the largest cities and even winter Olympic requirements have led to a shift away from small remote centers (e.g. Lake Placid, Lillehammer) as Olympic venues to larger cities (e.g. Turin, Vancouver) or at least sites adjacent to such cities. It is not only the urban infrastructure and services that are required to support the Olympics but the Olympic sites themselves (e.g. arenas and stadiums) that require large populations to make them viable on a long-term basis.

The City as Fortified Space

Fear and security increasingly dominate life in post-modern cities. Surveillance and policing have become dominant themes in the "carceral city" which has become a series of fortified spaces. Surveillance cameras have become typical devices whereby activity is monitored as a means of controlling behaviour, protecting property and ensuring public safety.

The Olympics are both affected by this urban trend and contribute towards it. On the one hand, the security needs of the Olympics are a defence against fear of attack from those who want to use the event for their own purposes or who oppose it. The high-profile nature of the Olympics makes them (or their officials or participants) an accessible target if proper precautions are not taken. On the other hand, the security needs of the Olympics are also a result of the Olympic product itself, which the IOC works hard to create. The marketing of the Olympics and its heroes, the protection of its brand, the controversies within the IOC or the issues in which it becomes embroiled, have intensified the need for a host city with significant fortified space. The modern Olympics have become synonymous with high security requirements and considerable attention to various forms of policing. Olympic villages are not only fortified spaces but increasingly so are Olympic venues. Considerable attention is paid to protection of members of the Olympic family, volunteers undergo various forms of screening, and the use of the Olympic brand and symbols are under watchful surveillance. Police have developed elaborate methods for crowd control and restricting access, and the development of policing strategies is consuming ever increasing costs for cities hosting the Olympics.

The Post-modern City and Long-term Olympic Impacts

If the goal of cities is not just to host the Olympics as a one-off event but to improve the city in some more enduring way, then it is important to determine what kind of changes it supports (Chalkley & Essex, 1999). Infrastructural improvements can be detailed but what is proposed here is to identify how the Olympics, and especially Olympic structures, are related to the post-modern city in the post-event period. There will be no attempt to deal with all of the matters raised above but a select number of issues will be examined that emerged particularly in the post-Olympic period in Calgary.

The assumption that structures this analysis is that Olympic outcomes go far beyond sport and that, from an urban perspective, non-sporting outcomes may be even more important than the sporting outcomes.[1] Having more facilities in which athletes can be trained may be an outcome considered a legacy, but the demolition of low-cost housing to build a new Olympic venue is also an outcome but would not be considered a legacy. Persons interested in a city's new training facilities would make one evaluation of this impact whereas persons responsible for housing the poor might have a very different evaluation. In short, the urban impact of the Olympics is much more complex and mixed (not just positive) than a sporting perspective might suggest. It is also important to recognize the distinction between planned versus unplanned or unintended outcomes. The goal might have simply been to build a new Olympic facility with no intention of deliberately making people homeless in the neighbouring area but that may have been the unintended result. Acknowledging only primary impacts without also being attuned to secondary consequences provides misleading interpretations of Olympic outcomes.

The post-Olympic period is perhaps the most ignored phase in the Olympic cycle. Because, by definition, the focal point of the cycle is the Games themselves, the emphasis is always on the Olympics, and what occurs afterwards has the lowest priority. The Organizing Committee has been disbanded, politicians are replaced or move on to other issues, and even the media lose interest. Once the euphoria is over, the Olympics drops from the public agenda and it becomes an event in the past. Several issues can be identified that underscore the long-term impact of the Olympics in light of the urban themes identified above.

The Residual Marketing Value of Being a Former Host Olympic City

Presumably the primary marketing time for a host city is in the pre-event phase and during the Games itself (e.g. Mount & Leroux, 1994). But does being a former Olympic city have any value at all? There is evidence that there is some kind of residual benefit to having been a host city, but that this benefit drops off dramatically over time (Preuss, 2003; Ritchie & Lyon, 1991). Having been a host city allows a city to commemorate that fact through its inclusion as an historic marker in the city's history and for which there might be some global public recognition. There may be a halo effect to having been an Olympic city, but its value wears thin as time passes and public opinion is directed to new and perhaps more recent Olympic sites. A new generation of citizens both locally and internationally has no recollection of the event at this place at all. While a successful Games may produce nostalgia and many collective memories among some residents, there is minimal value in them for cities to use the Games as a marketing tool in the post-event period. While Calgary has signs at the entrance to the city commemorating the Games, the fact that the city has searched for other events of global proportions (e.g. a failed 2005 World Expo bid) to sustain the marketing thrust serves as evidence that the impact of the Olympics was waning.

Former Olympic facilities, though, do provide an interesting illustration of how the Olympic influence is both preserved and transformed. The naming rights of the Olympic Saddledome (the primary indoor ice event venue seating about 20,000 people) was sold to corporate interests and named in succession the Canadian Airlines Saddledome, and then the Pengrowth Saddledome with the "Olympic" designation totally removed. The Saddledome is the home arena for the city's National Hockey League team which receives considerable media exposure, but seldom is the linkage to the Olympics mentioned. On the other hand, the Olympic Oval on the university campus retains its name, presumably because its naming rights have less economic value. Both the Saddledome and Oval are signature structures for the city because of their size and visibility but the Oval receives much less publicity though it remains an active training/competition site for Olympic athletes in speedskating.

Canada Olympic Park (COP) which housed ski jumping and luge/bobsled on the edge of the city, however, has become a central piece in tourism marketing for the city. Located on a major highway 30 minutes from downtown, COP is unique in that it was a site for outdoor Olympic competition but within the boundaries of a major metropolitan city. Marketing itself as "the crown jewel of the XV Olympic Winter Games", the Park not only retains its Olympic name but also houses the Olympic Hall of Fame and Museum which celebrates the "glory" of the Calgary Olympics and other Canadian Winter Olympic achievements. It also continues as a training site for Olympic athletes in the competitions noted above. It has been argued by its management body (Calgary Olympic Development Authority) that COP is a tourist attraction that adds an additional day on to a visitor's stay in the city (although the evidence of that is waning). COP is the major remaining landmark in the city explicitly commemorating the Olympics and of continuing Olympic significance. While it is difficult to use former Olympic facilities as a way of "hard-branding" (Evans, 2003) a city (in the same way that a grand museum or "world's largest mall" might be able to do so), COP attempts to play a role in marketing the city as a tourist destination. The outline of the Saddledome in the Calgary skyline appears in many promotions of the city but, as already noted, its Olympic connection has been largely stripped away.

In sum, while there is some name recognition for the city of Calgary as a former host city at the global level, it has largely faded and remains only an historic benchmark. Furthermore, the facilities that were built for the Olympics and named accordingly have had mixed residual value in promoting the city. The hosting of occasional World Cup ski jump competitions and the legacy of the buildings as visible landmarks and training sites are important but have limited value as marketing tools for the city.

The Adaptation of Olympic Facilities for Post-Games Usage: Consumptive Leisure

Specialized competition facilities (e.g. velodromes, stadiums, speedskating ovals, etc.) might continue to host sport competitions or serve as training centres but not without a constant eye on requirements for upgrading to ensure the facility is at world standards. Many former Winter Olympic sites are allowed to fall into disrepair. The Olympic Oval in Calgary is one of only three indoor speedskating ovals in the world and is known to have very fast ice. Therefore it continues to attract athletes for training purposes as well as for World Cup competitions. Canada Olympic Park recently built "the world's only indoor year round" push start training facility for sliding sports known as the Ice House or National Sliding Centre. In an attempt to retain its place as a training facility for winter sport, largely due to its expensive refrigerated track, the Calgary Olympic Development Association (CODA) announced in 2002 its intention to establish Canada's first Canadian Centre of Sport Excellence (CCOSE) for which it needed CDN$260 million to ensure a state-of-the-art training facility which also would support research and new technologies. An FIS sanctioned Superpipe was also built for snow boarding and plans exist to build a water ramp for summer training for freestyle skiers. In other words, it was recognized that a former Olympic site must continue to reinvent itself and aggressively seek to retain its edge if it does not want to become obsolete.

But there are two other matters. One is that the demand on these sites for training or competitions was not significant enough to warrant its dedication only for that purpose. Second, on-going expenses meant that these facilities were expected to generate revenue, so they are rented out for both sport and non-sport uses. Stadiums and arenas have the greatest potential for multiple uses and revenue generation. For example, the Saddledome (located near the centre of the city) bills itself as "Calgary's leader for entertainment". "Today great seating, fabulous food, superior service, and state-of-the-art technology make the Saddledome the perfect choice for an unforgettable entertainment experience (website accessed June 2004)". COP advertises "wild slide rides" (luge or skeleton) at high speeds including a complete video analysis of your slide". Bobsleigh rides are advertised as "high banked corners and blinding straightaways" for $120 per person. Competitive sports facilities, then, are marketed for public consumption.

But if the description of these rides sounds more like a theme park, there are other aspects of the park that support consumptive leisure but also at a price. There is euro-bungee and wall climbing for a fee, the museum has a state-of-the-art theatre and Discovery Room "for hands-on fun", and a virtual reality hockey shootout game. There is mini golf, beach volleyball and softball diamonds for summer activity, and a 25k mountain bike trail (winter and summer). There is a retail shop for gifts and accessories, Sunday brunch at the Naturbahn Teahouse, tours of the park including rides on a glass elevator to the top of the 90-metre ski jump, and vacation packages with accommodations at an urban retreat and spa. Future plans are for the ski jump bowl to be transformed into an entertainment bowl that can seat 10,000. All of these activities have been developed since the Olympics and have been designed to increase revenue through leisure consumption. Future plans for a Festival Plaza, Athlete's Plaza and Centennial Plaza for COP all suggest the creation of even more of a theme park atmosphere.

There is a further problem related to the threat of obsolescence. In recent years, planning for post-Olympic usage has focused on designating a sum of money from Olympic revenues to assist in the on-going operation of Olympic facilities. But operational costs are quite different from structural redesign, major improvements and technical upgrading which involve huge cost outlays. Facilities that may have been state-of-the-art at one point in time may easily be considered outdated ten or 20 years later. Facility managers then are left with a real struggle about how they will reinvent themselves to find the funds to move forward. This is particularly an issue because the urgency of investment to prepare for the Games is over and there is little incentive for governments to provide new funding.

In Calgary, several Olympic Endowment Funds were established after the Olympics (Warren & West, 2003) but this was hardly enough to make redesign changes or major repairs (e.g. the expensive leaking roof of the speedskating oval). CODA knew that if it wanted COP to continue to serve as a world-class training site that it would have to make some structural improvements. The way in which this was done was by proposing to establish a National Centre of Sport Excellence, a thematic rationale that allowed it to appeal to the government for new funding as well as to justify an appeal to the private sector for funds. The concern was not only to update the facilities but to ensure that the competitive advantage that the city had as a training site was maintained. The post-Olympic construction of the Superpipe, the Sliding Centre, and more recently a Gymnastics Centre represented an explicit attempt to prevent the erosion of the site as a unique training centre. This particularly became important in view of the fact that Vancouver won the bid for the 2010 Winter Games. If Vancouver's training/competition facilities became superior, then Calgary's facilities automatically would become nothing but an historic relic. All of this illustrates how the long-term future of the facilities must be related to standards of sporting excellence for which the bar is constantly being raised and which requires new investment or the facilities run the risk of becoming dated and obsolete. Obsolescence virtually eliminates the site from use by high performance athletes and reduces its significance for spectators and tourists as well.

The Issue of Public Expenditures and Social Exclusion

Almost all Olympic facilities are built using public funds. Restricting their use for elite sport must be counter-balanced with a desire to also make them accessible to the general public. This particularly becomes an issue in the post-Olympic period. Two interesting but very different examples in Calgary have been the open air Olympic Plaza in the downtown, on the one hand, and the Olympic Saddledome, Speedskating Oval and COP on the other hand. The Saddledome is used primarily by persons who purchase tickets for events, such as concerts and hockey games for which the renter charges an admission fee. Because of the cost of renting the facility and the cost of the entertainment provided, admission charges are always high meaning that public accessibility to the building is limited. In contrast, the Oval surface can be viewed from a visitors' gallery on the inside without charge, and the ice surface or the surrounding track can be used for a small fee. Canada Olympic Park plays a significant role as a training facility for young skiers who come with their school classes for which there is also a nominal fee. Summer camps, mountain bike racing, tours, etc. are also available to the public but always at a charge. Thus while COP is a "park", it is a private park that opens itself to the public but for a fee.

On the other hand, the Olympic Plaza which is located downtown is a public park with no barriers. Created as the site where medals were awarded each evening during the Olympics, and as a place to honour citizens of the city who paid to have their names inscribed on bricks, the Plaza is a very important *urban* legacy of the Olympics because of its role as a central city gathering place. Bounded by City Hall, the Centre for the Performing Arts, the Convention Centre, the Glenbow Museum and historic structures such as a cathedral, public art (the Famous Five), and former banks (now converted into restaurants), the Plaza provides open space for leisure in the heart of the downtown. The plaza has become a central location for community celebrations of many kinds and is often the site of concerts and other activities such as the International Children's Festival ("the happiest place in town"), skating (winter) and wading (summer), and an entertainment zone (Rope Square) during the annual Calgary Stampede summer festival. But it has also been the site of protest such as during the World Petroleum Congress and the G8 Summit in which surveillance increased dramatically and police presence was extremely high. The accessibility of the Plaza also means that homelessness and loitering have become issues which also increase surveillance. The Plaza is very close to the facilities that assist homeless people which ironically might also make it "the saddest place in town". However, in keeping with the urban theme of leisure consumption, surrounding businesses have banded together to use the Plaza as a way of marketing their businesses as the "Olympic Plaza Cultural District"—a cluster of 54 restaurants, bars and coffee shops within a two-block radius in support of five performing arts theatres, art galleries and a museum. It is clear then that the Plaza often becomes contested space in which the poor struggle for a place with those who link the space to more consumptive activity.

In contrast to Calgary, the medal ceremonies in Salt Lake City took place downtown in empty parking lots which were refurbished with temporary structures and then dismantled after the Games. Desiring to have a place where volunteers and local sponsors could be honored, an Olympic Legacy Plaza was created after the Olympics with a unique Olympic Snowflake Fountain featuring dancing waters, music and a wall inscribed with the names of 28,000 Olympic volunteers. However, the location of this unique feature was in a shopping and entertainment district known as the Gateway, a private commercial development in an old part of the city that was rejuvenated just in time for the Olympics. The Gateway consists of 90 stores and restaurants, a planetarium, 12 movie theatres, and condos and apartments. The Olympic Plaza, then, was linked to consumptive leisure and supported the embourgeoisment of inner-city space. Other than artwork or signage scattered throughout the downtown, this Plaza is the primary marker of the Olympics in the central city.[2]

Olympic facilities and sites built with public money must be protected and maintained, which establishes a quandary for their managers. Users paying fees help to deal with that problem. On the other hand, user charges serve as a basis for exclusion—a clear characteristic of the post-modern city. Public space is most closely allied with the interests of consumption industries and the public legacy of the Olympics seems to be easily linked to these activities.

The Impact of Olympic Facilities on Urban Form

As a foothills city in the Rocky Mountains of western Canada, Calgary was awarded the Olympics and hosted the Olympics during a time of tremendous population growth. This growth has continued (to now more than one million residents) particularly because Calgary serves as the headquarters for an ever-expanding Canadian and international oil and gas industry. Calgary is then a relatively young city that has grown significantly since the mid-1970s. While the concept of rapid transit seemed premature for a city this size at the time, the first leg of the light rail transit (LRT) became operative in 1981, which meant that the transportation needs of an extending city fit well with the transportation needs of the Olympics. The Olympic Saddledome, the Olympic Plaza, and the main Olympic Village all were located on the LRT line. It also meant that persons staying on the outskirts of the metropolitan area had convenient public transportation to major Olympic events. Other events, such as curling or NOC hospitality suites, were scattered throughout the city again reaffirming the fact that the Olympics require a large metropolitan area to accommodate all of its needs.

The preparation for the Olympics occurred at a time when the city was growing and, at least in some respects, this made the Olympics an important symbol for an ascendant city. The city needed a major indoor entertainment and ice centre anyway so that the construction of the Saddledome for the Olympics dovetailed nicely with urban needs. An expanding university needed more housing as well so the placement of the Athletes' Village at that location received strong support. The point is that many of the facilities required for the Olympics were recognized as imperative for the city anyway which reduced the sense of controversy that the Olympics provoked.

Another one of the issues which we have identified is how Olympic facilities have an impact on adjacent communities. This is a neglected aspect of Olympic impact analysis. Because many Winter Olympic events are held in the mountains, it is sometimes assumed that the urban impact of the Games in this manner is reduced in comparison to the Summer Games. Nevertheless, two illustrations from Calgary can be given which demonstrate how the Winter Olympics can affect urban form.

The Olympic Saddledome was built within an older inner-city community bordering the central business district in an area called Victoria Park East. The construction of this building played a role in the continuing deterioration of the area as a residential community and its eventual collapse (Hiller, 2000). In the first instance, the fast-track construction required for quick action to prove to the IOC that Calgary was a serious contender in the Olympic bid skipped the usual hearings and consultations with the community which had long experienced conflict with the city and developers. The question was whether the community of largely single detached homes should be preserved as a low-density area or whether it should experience urban renewal with much higher density development. This residential area was also located adjacent to the Stampede grounds where the world-famous Calgary Stampede is held every year and where the Saddledome was to be built. The Stampede had their own goals to make the grounds into a year-round entertainment centre, and expansion into the residential area would have to occur to accommodate the Saddledome. As the community continued to deteriorate due to its uncertain future, the family-oriented residents moved out and these residents were replaced by low-income renters in a rooming house configuration. Redevelopment of the residential area then meant the dislocation of the poor, and this process also continued after the Olympics to accommodate other Stampede plans for expansion. It is significant to note that, again, it was leisure consumption that allied Olympic development with Stampede goals. Since the Olympics, almost all of the poor have been displaced, and the area is ready for both its growing entertainment role and the gentrification of the community.

Canada Olympic Park also has plans to expand as an activity and entertainment centre and has purchased another 300 acres (which doubles the size of this site) to accommodate its future plans. However, this property known as Paskapoo Slopes is environmentally sensitive and requires a series of hearings before further development is allowed. Adjacent residential communities are also somewhat concerned about how COP's plans will affect them. These examples demonstrate that after-use can have a continuing and even more intrusive impact on neighbouring communities long after the Olympics are over, especially as adjustments are made to ensure the viability of the facilities. Displacement effects or the re-evaluation of property are both matters that ought to be part of the research agenda in the post-Olympic period.

Conclusion

There is no question that there is a sporting outcome for a city in hosting the Olympics. Maintaining event facilities at world standards in the post-event period can continue to give the city an international profile, at least in the sporting world (e.g. Calgary hosted the World Figure Skating Championships in 2006). However, after the Olympics, the use of Olympic facilities must be re-evaluated and integrated into the fabric of urban life and the needs of its residents. To the extent that Winter Olympic facilities are based in cities, the evidence, after almost two decades, in Calgary is that the post-Olympic use of Games' facilities are primarily playing a role in supporting the post-modern turn towards leisure consumption as a marker of urban life.

References

Andranovich, G., Burbank, M. J., & Heying, C. H. (2001). Olympic cities: lessons from mega-event politics. *Journal of Urban Affairs*, 23(2), 113–131.

Cashman, R. (2006). *The Bitter-sweet Awakening: The Legacy of the Sydney 2000 Olympic Games*. Petersham, Australia: Walla Walla Press.

Chalkley, B., & Essex, S. (1999). Urban development through hosting international events: History of the Olympic Games. *Planning Perspectives*, 14(4), 369–394.

Clark, T. N. (2004). *The City as an Entertainment Mmachine*. Amsterdam: Elsevier.

Espy, R. (1979). *The Politics of the Olympic Games*. Berkeley, CA: University of California Press.

Essex, S., & Chalkley, B. (1998). Olympic Games: Catalyst of urban change. *Leisure Studies*, 17, 187–206.

Evans, G. (2003). Hard-branding the cultural city. *International Journal of Urban and Regional Research*, 27, 417–440.

Gratton, C., & Henry, I. P. (2001). *Sport in the City: The Role of Sport in Economic and Social Regeneration*. New York: Routledge.

Hall, T., & Hubbard., P. (1998). *The Entrepreneurial City: Geographies of Politics, Regime, and Representation*. Chichester: John Wiley.

Hannigan, J. (1998). *Fantasy City: Pleasure and Profit in the Post-modern Metropolis*. New York: Routledge.

Harvey, D. (1988). From managerialism to entrepreneurialism: The transformation of governance in late capitalism. *Geografiska Annaler*, 7113, 3–17.

Hiller, H. H. (1998). Assessing the impact of mega-events: A linkage model. *Current Issues in Tourism*, 1(1), 47–57.

Hiller, H. H. (1999). Toward an urban sociology of mega-events. *Research in Urban Sociology*, 5, 181–205.

Hiller, H. H. (2000). Mega-events and community obsolescence: Redevelopment vs. rehabilitation in Victoria Park East. *Canadian Journal of Urban Research*, 8(1), 47–81.

Hiller, H. H. (2003). Toward a science of Olympic outcomes: The urban legacy. In M. de Moragas, C. Kennett, & N. Puig (Eds.), *The Legacy of the Olympic Games 1984–2000*(pp. 102–109). Lausanne: IOC.

Kennett, C., & Moragas, M. de. (2006). Barcelona 1992: Evaluating the Olympic legacy. In A. Tomlinson, & C. Young (Eds.), *National Identity and Global Sports Events*(pp. 177–219). Albany, NY: State University of New York Press.

Lenskyj, H. J. (2000). *Inside the Olympic Industry: Power, Politics, Activism*. Alban, NY: State University of New York Press.

Moragas, M. de, & Botella, M. (1995). *Keys to Success: The Social, Sporting, Economic and Communications*. Impact of Barcelona '92. Barcelona: Centre for Olympic Studies.

Mount, J., & Leroux, C. (1994). Assessing the effects of a mega-event: a retrospective study of the impact of the Olympic games on the Calgary business sector. *Festival Management and Event Tourism: An International Journal*, 2, 15–23.

Preuss, H. (2003). Rarely considered economic legacies of Olympic games. In M. de Moragas, C. Kennett, N. Puig, & N. (Eds.), *The Legacy of the Olympic Games 1984–2000*(pp. 243–252). Lausanne: IOC.

Preuss, H. (2004). *The Economics of Staging the Olympics: A Comparison of the Games, 1972–2008*. Cheltenham, UK: Edward Elgar.

Ritchie, J. R. B., & Lyons, M. (1991). The impact of mega-events on host region awareness: A longitudinal study. *Journal of Travel Research*, 30(1), 3–10.

Roche, M. (2001). *Mega-events and Modernity: Olympics and Expos in the Growth of Global Culture*. New York: Routledge.

Searle, G. (2003). The urban legacy of the Sydney Olympic games. In M. de Miquel, C. Kennett, & N. Puig (Eds.), *The Legacy of the Olympic Games 1984–2000* (pp. 118–126). Lausanne: IOC.

Smyth, H. (1994). *Marketing the City: The Role of Flagship Developments in Urban Regeneration*. London: E & F N Spon.

Soja, E. W. (2001). Exploring the post-metropolis. In C. Minca (Ed.), *Post-modern Geography: Theory and Praxis*(pp. 37–56). Oxford: Blackwell.

Warren, L., & West, J. T. (2003). Calgary and the legacy of the XV Olympic Winter Games. In M. de Moragas, C. Kennett, & N. Puig (Eds.), *The Legacy of the Olympic Games 1984–2000* (pp. 170–178). Lausanne: IOC.

Whitson, D., & MacIntosh, D. (1996). The global circus: International sport, tourism and the marketing of cities. *Journal of Sport and Social Issues*, 23, 278–295.

Zukin, S. (1995). *The Culture of Cities*. Cambridge: Blackwell.

The Sports Development Potential of Sports Event Volunteering: Insights from the XVII Manchester Commonwealth Games

PAUL M. DOWNWARD* & RITA RALSTON**

*School of Sport and Exercise Sciences, Loughborough University, UK, **Manchester Metropolitan University, UK

Public investment in sports facilities and events is a widely debated topic in sports management and economics. Debate concerns the use of sports investment as an economic policy intervention that yields potential benefits to a community following the use of public funds to construct stadia and facilities and/or to host sports events. Consequently, the literature focuses on the purported direct and indirect economic benefits and costs. Less is written about the intangible economic impacts, and even less on the 'human legacy'. This paper attempts to contribute to filling this gap in the literature by exploring the sports development impacts upon the interest in sport, sports participation and sports volunteering, as well impacts upon more general volunteering that follow from the experience of volunteering at a major sporting event, the XVII Manchester Commonwealth Games. This implies viewing the investment in a major event as a sports development and social policy tool as much as an economic intervention per se.

The next section of the paper briefly reviews some of the main themes in the literature examining the tangible and intangible economic impacts of investment in sport. A brief review of the literature on sports volunteering is then undertaken, to highlight the differential nature of sports-events volunteers and the potential links between event and more regular sports volunteering and participation as a form of sports 'career' progression. The data employed in the research are then presented. Subsequently, both descriptive and inferential statistical analyses are presented to explore how experiences of volunteering at a major event affects sports development and non-sport volunteering. Conclusions and policy discussion then follow.

The Economic Impact of Sports Investment

Most of the literature evaluating investment in sports has focused upon the economic case for justifying public subsidy of sports infrastructure and events rather than the impact upon human resources. In particular, there is a burgeoning literature that addresses stadium redevelopment in US professional team sports (Baade, 2003). The valuation of the beneficial impacts has been repeatedly stated in a variety of ex-ante multiplier studies, typically undertaken by consultancy firms for pro-stadium lobbyists. However, the academic literature assessing these claims ex post has cast doubt upon the reliability of the calculations in the literature and also the economic case for the public subsidy of sport investment (Baade, 1996; Baade & Dye, 1990; Baade & Matheson, 2004; Coates & Humphreys, 1999; Crompton, 1995; Hudson, 2001; Siegfried & Zimbalist, 2000). Although the literature is less developed in the UK, and does not address professional team sports, in a review of 16 sports events Gratton *et al.* (2005) argue that, despite there being obvious economic benefits to the host communities, the key issue concerns the source of funding of these investments. Consequently, net transfers into a community appear worth it from a local perspective, but are not necessarily so from a national perspective as the *best* use of public funds. Consequently it is also argued that despite these event-specific evaluations, there is little evidence about the medium- to long-term economic effects of such sports event-led economic regeneration strategies.

In such an environment it is not surprising that Crompton (2004) has argued that there is a need to shift away from the conventional economic assessment of the impact of sports investment and instead to focus upon the "psychic income" generated. Crompton (2004) argues that psychic income stems from the emotional and psychological benefits received by host communities from their being associated with a sports event. This contrasts with the literal income generated by the increased spending associated with, for example, visitors to the event.

Environmental valuation measures, such as contingent valuation, can be used to evaluate psychic income to identify the "willingness to pay" for the existence of (or the option of attending) the sports event (see, for example, Downward, 2004). Theoretically speaking this involves an attempt to value the consumer surplus associated with a non-priced resource. It is clear that Crompton's strategy offers an alternative potential policy option for those seeking to explore the wider economic effects of sports event or facility investment.

However, it is clear that in exploring the sports development impact of investment in facilities or events, matters are more complicated. In the discussion above, the traditional emphasis is primarily associated with exploring the impacts of potential spectators spending money at the events, or measuring the community's psychic income that follows from a latent demand for sports investment. There is a presumption that the underlying structure of demand is unchanged. Yet, if a sports event is being used as a policy intervention to change behaviour then this assumption is not realistically met. A change in the motivation and expectations of individuals, that is their preferences, say, for subsequent sports participation, is indicative of this.

As Downward *et al.* (2005) argue, the same would be true following changes to the social structure within which choices were made. This is particularly important for volunteers for, as Moreno *et al.* (2000) argue, volunteering is linked to the formation of social structures because they harness collective motivation and action. It is clear, thus, that in investigating the human legacy of sports events such potential changes in behaviour need to be investigated. Prior to discussing this issue, however, it is important to understand something of the current structure of volunteering decisions. As well as illustrating the potential for using sports events as sports policy interventions it helps in assessing the reliability of the current research.

Sports Volunteering

Burgham and Downward (2005), Downward *et al.* (2005) and Ralston *et al.* (2004) review sports volunteering profiles in the UK, with sports volunteering here defined by Gratton *et al.* (1997) as:

> ... individual volunteers helping others in sport, in a formal organization such as clubs or governing bodies, and receiving either no remuneration or only expenses. (p. i)

The general literature on volunteering reveals that 26% of all volunteers were formally involved in sport. The time that they spent volunteering had, moreover, risen from 2.7 hours in 1991 to an average of 4.05 hours a week in 1997 (Davis-Smith, 1998). Yet, as discussed by Nichols (2004, 2005), older cohorts are sustaining volunteer activity in the UK. For example, those aged 45–54 volunteered the most, followed by retired people aged 65–74.

The national surveys also tend to reveal that males and females volunteer equally but are much more likely to be drawn from the White British ethnic group and from higher socioeconomic groupings. Volunteers are also likely to have higher education levels, to be married or cohabiting, and have children and access to a car and a community network. As far as sports volunteering is concerned, the research reveals that this is more likely to be undertaken by male and younger volunteers.

The specific literature on sport volunteering refines these insights in the context of both individual sports and sports events. Sport England (2003), confirms that in regular individual sports, approximately two-thirds of volunteers are male as opposed to female. So too, more formal activities are typically carried out by older volunteers, with most having no dependent children. Whilst four hours is identified as the average weekly duration of volunteering, moreover, these increase in volunteering activity for National Governing Bodies and clubs. The increased formalities associated with volunteering is also suggestive of a male orientation of sports volunteering, as males are much more likely to be the chairperson, or treasurer of clubs, as well as holding senior coaching positions.

Likewise in regular festivals and events, the research suggests that volunteers tend to reflect the gender and age profile of the participants in the sports involved (see, for example, Harrington *et al.*, 2000) but the larger and more unique the event, the broader the volunteer profiles (see Chalip, 2000; MacAloon, 2000; Moreno *et al.* 2000 in the context of the Olympics). This implies that the increased regularity of events could be linked to the development of a body of volunteers that develops core competences in running the event thus ensuring its sustainability (Coyne & Coyne, 2001; Farrell *et al.*, 1998).

One important implication of this is that it suggests a potential career profile of sports volunteering, and/or participation in line with Stebbins' (1982) concept of serious leisure. Accordingly, casual involvement in a particular event may then lead the individual to progress to regular volunteering or participation in a specific sport. Clearly this is of extreme importance to policy makers seeking to use sports events as sports development policy instruments. The relevance of the concept cannot be presumed, however, particularly given that the evidence reviewed above tends to show that there is a historic distinction from mixed cohorts of volunteers at particular events to male domination in specific sports.

There is also no straightforward relationship between participation and volunteering. Indeed, often sports with wide participation require less formal organization and age can prevent participation (Coleman, 2002; Gratton *et al.* 1997). The dynamics of change are thus likely to be complex. It is with these issues in mind, therefore, that the current research is offered. A large-scale mega-event, such as the Commonwealth Games, offers the opportunity to explore the potential for sports events to raise interest, participation and volunteering in sport as a human legacy of sports investment.

Figure 1 provides an indication of the empirical relationships investigated in this research. Drawing upon Burgham & Downward (2005), and

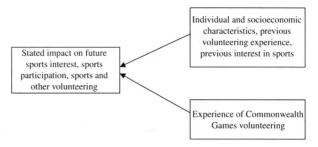

Figure 1. Determinants of Sports Development

Downward (forthcoming) it is postulated that volunteering in sport, or participating in sport, emerges from a set of individual, economic, social and sports characteristics. These characteristics may refer to a number of different theoretical concepts, such as the income–time constraints of economics, or sports literacy facilitated by previous involvement in sport (see Green *et al.*, 2005). However, these characteristics are now augmented by the experiences of volunteering, as discussed above in connection with the concept of serious leisure.

Context, Data and Variables

The current research focuses on the Crew 2002 volunteers of the XVII Manchester Commonwealth Games and draws upon a broader research project, which was a collaborative venture with UK Sport and the Manchester 2002 Volunteer Programme (M2002), sponsored by Adecco, a major recruitment company. As part of a quantitative investigation of issues associated with volunteering, the research involved the use of a question-naire to elicit information on volunteer socioeconomic background, their current volunteering experience, experiences of the Games and also the stated likely impacts of their experience on their interest in sport, and future likely participation and volunteering behaviour.[1] The sample frame selected comprised the database of 9,000 volunteers. Every seventh person was selected from the database giving a sample of 1,300 volunteers. A judgement was made that the approach would not be easily biased as the database was not organized by any particular volunteer characteristic other than alphabetical order of name. Following the Games, the questionnaire was issued in May 2003 and 407 replies were obtained.

As the main aim of the research was to identify the sports development implications associated with experience of volunteering at the Common-wealth Games it is important to note that, in line with the research strategy above, data were collected according to the categories of the conceptual model detailed in Figure 1. To reiterate, this postulates that the experiences of the Games in the light of the individual and socioeconomic characteristics of respondents would affect the stated future behaviour of volunteers with respect to their interest in sport, sports participation, and volunteering and subsequent volunteering.

Most variables were measured as a series of nominal values including sex, age ethnicity, health and employment status, and previous experience as a volunteer. Previous interest and participation in sport was measured on a five-point Likert scale with 5 indicating *strongly agree* and 1 indicating *strongly disagree* measuring the strength of agreement, or disagreement, with a statement concerning these issues. The same was the case with the large number of dimensions of the experience of the Games that were investigated. Each of these statements sought to explore potential dimensions of experience that were associated with changes to personal or social capital, enjoyment and social satisfaction, task satisfaction, as well as specific experiences of the work tasks that were undertaken.

Finally, Table 1 indicates the statements that were used to investigate the sports development and other implications of experience as a volunteer. They can be treated as the dependent variables in the subsequent analysis. The dependent variables are numbered in the first column from '1' to '16', which are used to indicate the relevant regression results in Table 1. Once again, respondents were asked to indicate their agreement or disagreement on a five-point Likert scale, anchored as above, with 5 indicating *strongly agree* and 1 indicating *strongly disagree*.

Results

The remaining columns of Table 1 present some initial descriptive results on the variables measuring the development implications of volunteering at the Games. They can be viewed as unconditional statements of the impacts of volunteering.

The results reveal that while there is evidence of some increase in interest in sport and particularly a wider range of sports, as a result of the respondents' experience of volunteering at the Games, there is no strong evidence that this will translate into more participation or volunteering in specific sports. For example, only between about 6–14% of the sample may increase participation, or 12–21% of the sample actually volunteer for more sports and 8–17% of the sample intend to increase their hours of volunteering.

Similar patterns apply for non-sports volunteering. Approximately 14% of the sample suggest that they intend to volunteer in new contexts and 23% that they actually volunteer in new contexts. However, approximately 43% of the sample indicate greater interest in volunteering generally and approximately 57% greater awareness of volunteering opportunities, with approximately 46% of the sample indicating more likelihood of their approaching organizations in order to volunteer. Finally, there is strong evidence of willingness to volunteer for another major sports event, or another major event.

There are a number of implications of these results. The first is that they suggest that mechanical notions that investment in sports events will simply raise sports interest, participation and volunteering, as human legacies, are misplaced. Relatively small proportions of the sample suggest this possibi-

Table 1. Unconditional Outcomes of Games Volunteering

	Strongly agree %	Agree %	Neutral %	Disagree %	Strongly disagree %	n
Interest (model number)						
I am now more interested in sport (1)	3.2	17.9	28	36.5	14.4	403
I am now more interested in a wider range of sport (2)	5.2	39.5	18.4	25.6	11.4	403
Participation						
I now participate in sport more (3)	1.2	5.5	26.6	45.9	20.8	403
I now participate in new sports (4)	1.5	4.5	19.4	51.6	23.1	403
I intend to participate more often in sport (5)	2.2	11.7	27.8	40	18.4	403
I intend to participate in a wider range of sports (6)	1	12.9	25.8	41.4	18.9	403
Sport volunteering						
I do more hours as a sports volunteer (7)	2.3	6	17.5	44.6	29.5	383
I intend to do more hours as a sports volunteer (8)	1.6	15.4	32	31	20	384
I now volunteer for new sports (9)	1.6	10.7	20.6	41.1	26	384
I intend to volunteer for new sports (10)	1.8	19.5	24.5	32.8	21.4	384
I am willing to volunteer for another major sports event (11)	46.6	39	10.8	2.2	1.5	408
Non-sport volunteering						
I actually volunteer in a wider range of activities/organizations (12)	3.8	11.8	21.1	43.6	19.8	399
I now intend to volunteer in a wider range of activities organizations (13)	3.0	19.8	29.1	31.6	16.5	399
I am now more interested in voluntary work generally (14)	6.7	36.1	23.9	21.6	11.7	402
I am more aware of a wider range of opportunities (15)	7	49.5	19.9	17.4	6.2	402
I am willing to volunteer for another major event (16)	26.3	41.4	22.8	6.2	3.2	403

lity. This has implications for sports policy and management, which are discussed more fully later. The second, is that taken at face value these results might be expected as part of the serious leisure hypothesis of volunteer career progression as discussed earlier. That is, experience of irregular event volunteering consolidates any interest in sport and that this needs to be capitalized upon to promote specific sports participation and volunteering. One complication with this conclusion, however, is that Table 3 also reveals a stronger impact of experience of the Games upon non-sports volunteering that might be suggestive of the Games more likely impact upon wider social capital that does not reflect sport infrastructure. Consequently to explore these issues further, more probing empirical work is required.

To facilitate this, a factor analysis of the experiences of the Games was first undertaken to identify common, systematic aspects of the experience of volunteering at the Games. The data matrix proved amenable to a factor analysis as indicated by the Bartlett test for sphericity, which was significant at the .000 level. Factor loadings of 0.4 were treated as significant in keeping with the literature (see, for example, Hair *et al.*, 1990). A principal components analysis was used, such that extracted factors, as indicated by their eigenvalues, accounted for at least as much variance as the items measuring the experiences of volunteers as detailed in Table 2. These items, of course, can be thought of as potential individual variables in their own right. An orthogonal rotation was also used to minimise the collinearity between the factors because they were to be used in subsequent regression analysis. Initially 15 factors were identified. However, a number of the items measuring the experiences of volunteering was significant on more than one factor. These are detailed in Table 2. Consequently these items were dropped from the analysis. The subsequent factor analysis produced 13 factors accounting for 67.2% of the variance in the data. However, despite Cronbach's alpha statistics reporting that they were reliable scales, most of these comprised two items or less. Consequently, it was decided to focus on five main factors accounting for 48.1% of the total variance that comprised more items.

The first column presents the items measuring the experiences of volunteering that were included in the analysis. The subsequent columns present the five extracted factors and their significant factor loadings. The Cronbach alpha statistic, the eigenvalue and percentage of variance for each factor are reported at the bottom of each column. The five factors measure dimensions of experience associated with the organization of volunteering experienced, personal development, the assignments undertaken, helping the community surrounding the Games and the opportunity to see the event and meet celebrities.

Second, an ordered Logit regression analysis used the factors above and the variables measuring individual and socioeconomic characteristics of volunteers as regressors exploring the statements concerning interest in sport, participation and volunteering in sport, and non-sport volunteering as a result of volunteering at the Games.[2] Clearly, the latter characteristics affect the potential capacity that volunteers have to change their behaviour

Table 2. Factor Analysis of Volunteer Experiences

Experience\factor	1	2	3	4	5
I got clear instructions on what I am supposed to be doing	.690				
I was fully trained by the time the games started	.672				
Everything ran smoothly	.647				
The managers knew what they were doing	.771				
My team leader was well organized	.813				
My team leader had good people management skills	.790				
My efforts were always appreciated	.667				
Volunteers and paid staff were treated as equals	.584				
Rotas were well planned	.618				
Shifts were of the right length	.512				
Communication between volunteers and M2002 was good	.605				
Communication between volunteers and team leaders was good	.804				
It improved my chances of employment		.543			
It looks good on my CV and application forms		.570			
I have learned new skills and capabilities		.793			
I enhanced developed my skills		.773			
I have enhanced my personal development		.868			
I have increased my self-confidence		.846			
It has provided new challenges		.764			
It has changed my life		.654			
I was happy with my assigned location			.869		
I was happy with my assigned venue			.804		
I was happy with my assigned work area			.854		
I was happy with my assigned task			.819		
Overall, I was happy with the assignment			.842		
I met interesting people			.454		
I was part of a team			.410		
I did something interesting every day			.451		
I helped Manchester				.842	
I helped the north-west				.885	
I showed support for my country				.638	
I got the chance to see some of the main events					.562
I saw some of the celebrities and sports stars					.832
I saw a lot of famous people					.786
The spectators treated me with respect					.432
I was bored and it gave me something to do					
I did something different from my usual work					
I enjoyed wearing a uniform and having official status					
There were some perks or free gifts					
I supported sport					
It highlighted that we should be less money motivated and do something for society					
I set an example for my children/grandchildren					
It has been a great conversation piece					
Some days I was so tired I could have slept standing up					

Table 2 (*Continued*)

Experience\factor	1	2	3	4	5
Some days I didn't know if I was coming or going					
There were times when I was really cross and bad tempered					
There were times when the other volunteers got on my nerves					
I wasn't left out of pocket					
If I didn't like what I saw I soon let them know					
They expected too much from me: I was only working on a voluntary basis					
It was a chance of a lifetime					
I made useful business contacts					
Volunteer meals were satisfactory					
Transport for volunteers was good					
Cronbach's alpha	0.912	0.902	0.905	0.856	0.774
Eigenvalues	13.356	5.261	2.848	2.502	1.992
Percentage of variance	24.734	9.743	5.274	4.634	3.689

Notes:
Factor names
  1. Organization
  2. Personal development
  3. Assignment
  4. Community
  5. Celebrities
Deleted items
  1. It was an exciting experience
  2. I did something useful for the community
  3. It gave me satisfaction to help others
  4. I enjoyed every moment of it
  5. I have memories to treasure for the rest of my life
  6. I used my skills
  7. The selection process matched my assigned role with my skills

and must be accounted for. Moreover, in the regression analyses robust (Huber–White) standard errors were employed to establish statistical significance to allow for any heteroscedasticity in the samples.[3]

Table 3 provides the regression results for each of the types of development explored: sports interest, sports participation, sports volunteering and non-sports volunteering. The dependent variable is implied at the top of columns 2 onwards in the table, with the stated number corresponding to the statement detailed in Table 1. The independent variables, or regressors, are detailed in the first column. At the bottom of each table the sample size of each regression is indicated as 'N'. The 'pseudo R^2' is presented as appropriate to ordered logit analysis along with the corresponding Wald test statistic, which tests the null hypothesis that the pseudo

R^2 is equal to zero. In all but three cases this value is significant at the 5% level, suggesting that the broader model has some relevance.[4] What appears as low values of the Pseudo R^2 compared to the equivalent R^2 for ordinary least squares regression should be viewed with caution. As Long and Freese (2003) indicate, in regression models for categorical dependent variables, a variety of pseudo R^2 are available, these tend to have low values, ranging between 0.2 and 0.4, and should be best viewed in relative comparison than absolute size. The values reported in this research, as lower than this range, suggest that more explanation is possible. However, because of the differential nature of pseudo R^2, Stata (2003) argues that it is best to focus on the Wald statistic in assessing the model. Columns 2 onwards of each table indicate the estimated partial slope coefficients for each variable and, beneath it, in brackets, the asymptotic Z-value. For ease of interpretation, significant variables at the 5% level only are reported.[5]

Columns 1 and 2 reveal that relative to other ages, middle-aged volunteers are less likely to have developed more interest in a wider range of sports. However, the personal development elements of the event-volunteer experience, identified by the factor analysis, do raise interest in sport and a wider range of sports. Notably too, a wider range of interest is noted for those who previously attended sports events. This is evidence of volunteering at a major event exposing volunteers to new experiences as previous attendance at sports events is most likely to be with specific sports, as discussed earlier. Previous volunteering experience is insignificant.

Columns 3 to 6 explore the actual increases, or intention to increase, in sports participation in terms of current frequency of participation or participation in new sports. The evidence suggests that, relative to the young, this is less likely, particularly for those in middle-age. However, actual participation in new sports may rise for those in employment or are retired. This is perhaps indicative of the income or time needed to explore new pursuits as implied in the income leisure trade-off model (Burgham & Downward, 2005; Downward, 2004; Gratton & Taylor, 2000). On the one hand, rising incomes are often associated with financial access to sport, on the other hand, rising incomes can be associated with greater time commitments. The results also show that previously watching sports on TV can work against promoting participation. However, there is some evidence that those who attend sports events now have greater intentions to participate in sport more, or a wider range of sports.

In terms of specific experiences of volunteering at the Games, it is clear that enhancements to the personal development of volunteers promotes participation or its intention. However, there is some evidence that organizational, assignment and community experiences of volunteering, as identified in the factor analysis, may counter increases in participation. This is evidence of the complex effects of sports events. Each of these negative influences on participation is associated with positive experiences associated with the organization of their volunteering activity, the tasks undertaken and the sense of rewarding their community. Consequently, they are indicative of some incentive facing the volunteers to shift away from active sports participation towards facilitating sports for others as volunteers.

Columns 7 to 11 report results associated with actual increases in, or intentions to increase, sports volunteering. Naturally, in the case of volunteering more actual hours, previous sports volunteering is significant. This suggests some encouragement to deepen involvement in sports. However, once again there is a negative influence identified for experiences of the event assignment. This is also the case for volunteering for new sports. As discussed below this is indicative of a degree of enhanced interest in non-sports volunteering for current sports volunteers.

The results also show that previously attending sports events coupled with experiences of the Games raising personal development, can raise intentions to volunteer more hours. Relative to those in part-time or full-time

Table 3. Regression Analysis

Regressor\model	1	2	3	4	5	6	7	8
Sex								
Age2				−1.152				
				(−2.75)				
Age3		−1.172	−1.142	−1.465	−0.838	−1.05		
		(−2.71)	(−2.70)	(−3.52)	(−2.00)	(−2.2)		
Age4				−1.614				
				(−2.63)				
Ethwb								
Health								
Emp2			0.813	1.057				0.888
			(2.25)	(3.02)				(2.2)
Emp3				1.260				
				(2.57)				
Emp4								
Sportint								
Sportatt		0.286			0.338	0.294		
		(2.05)			(2.33)	(2.25)		
Sportwat			−0.356	−0.395	−0.361	−0.279		
			(−2.56)	(−2.50)	(−2.66)	(−1.96)		
Sportpar								
Volunt							0.709	
							(2.68)	
Organization			−0.003					
			(−2.44)					
Personal development	0.004	0.007	0.004	0.004	0.005	0.005		
	(3.32)	(4.90)	(3.43)	(2.74)	(3.95)	(3.55)		
Assignment					−0.003	−0.003	−0.003	−0.002
					(−2.49)	(−2.94)	(−2.28)	(−2.09)
Community			−0.003	−0.004		−0.003		
			(−2.79)	(−3.00)		(−2.21)		
Celebrities								
n	311	311	311	311	311	311	295	296
Pseudo R-squared	0.04	0.0857	0.0767	0.0765	0.0956	0.1018	0.0426	0.0398
Wald Chi-squared (25)	32.14	75.21	47.79	46.86	81.77	77.40	27.51	31.79
P >Chi-squared	0.0301	0.000	0.000	0.000	0.000	0.000	0.09	0.033

Table 3. (Continued)

Regressor\model	9	10	11	12	13	14	15	16
Sex				0.569 (2.33)				
Age2								
Age3			−0.954 (−2.18)		−0.897 (−2.20)			−0.953 (−2.37)
Age4		−1.589 (−2.7)						
Ethwb						0.929 (1.98)		
Health						−0.728 (−2.43)		
Emp2								
Emp3								
Emp4	1.058 (1.99)							
Sportint								
Sportatt		0.315 (2.12)	0.343 (2.79)					0.341 (2.38)
Sportwat					−0.283 (−2.22)			
Sportpar								−0.212 (−2.06)
Volunt				1.100 (4.47)				
Organization			0.003 (2.15)					
Personal development		0.003 (2.19)	0.003 (2.31)		0.003 (2.41)	0.004 (3.63)	0.003 (2.67)	0.003 (2.96)
Assignment								
Community								
Celebrities								
n	296	310	296	311	311	311	304	311
Pseudo R-squared	0.0355	0.0733	0.0491	0.0456	0.0432	0.0451	0.0366	0.04
Wald Chi-squared (25)	30.55	53.55	41.74	43.41	49.78	40.46	28.88	51.56
P > Chi-squared	0.045	0.000	0.002	0.001	0.000	0.003	0.0679	0.000

Notes: Sex: Male or Female; Age: Age categories; Ethwb: White British or not.
Health: Long-term health problem or not; Emp: Employment categories.
Volunt: Current involvement in voluntary work; Sportint, Sportatt, Sportwat, Sportpar: interest in sport, attending sports events, watching sport on T.V., participating in sport.

education, moreover, those in part-time or full-time employment are more likely to volunteer for new sports. Again, this is indicative of the threshold effects of income on involvement in sports as discussed above.

Finally, apart from the oldest volunteers, previous attendance at sports events, and the enhancement of personal development all suggest increased willingness to volunteer for another major sports event. This is suggestive that any trade-offs associated with event volunteering and previous sports participation and volunteering may be, at least, compensated by increased interest in volunteering for sports events.

Columns 12 to 16 review the impacts upon non-sport volunteering. There is some evidence that relative to the young, older age groups are less likely to; intend to volunteer in a wider range of activities or organizations or be more interested in voluntary work generally. These results suggest that there is broad evidence that younger volunteering is encouraged.

It is clear that in the case of actual volunteering in a wider range of activities or organizations, previous volunteering experience matters. Significantly too, males are more likely to volunteer in a wider range of activities. As males are more likely to be regular sports volunteers this is further evidence, as implied above, that sports event volunteering may develop non-sports volunteering interests more.

Further the personal development experience of volunteering at the Games is shown to promote intention to volunteer, interest in voluntary work, awareness of a wider range of opportunities for volunteering, and willingness to volunteer at another major event. Collectively, these are indications of the non-sport social capital enhancing potential of volunteer experiences developed through experience of sports events. In contrast, the results reveal that interest in watching sport on TV may reduce intentions to volunteer in a wider range of activities or organizations. Although, the latter is more likely for those who attend sports events. Finally, health problems reduce willingness to volunteer at another major event.

Summary and Policy Discussion

While there is clearly some variety and idiosyncracy in the above results, and despite there being a need to increase the explanatory power of the research, nonetheless some clear patterns do emerge when one views the results across the dependent variables. The results suggest that interest in sport is raised for younger volunteers, those feeling personally developed by their experience of volunteering at the Games, and those who attend sports events. Likewise, actual increases in participation in, and intentions to participate more, both in existing and in a wider range of sports is enhanced for those experiencing personal development from volunteering at the Games. Again, this is more likely to be the case for younger volunteers, and those who previously attended sports events. In contrast, this is less likely for those with a passive interest in sports, through watching on TV. There is also some evidence that to the extent that volunteers felt that they enhanced the community through their volunteering activity, or enjoyed their assignment while volunteering, then this could reduce active participation and volunteering respectively. There is an element of a trade off between facilitating and participating in sport.

Specifically, as far as sports volunteering is concerned, volunteer hours can increase for those currently involved in volunteering, with the intention to increase hours for those feeling personally developed and with previous attendance at sports events. Again, however, there is some evidence that good experiences of event volunteering may help to attenuate these increases.

The likely beneficiaries of these potential reductions in participation and more regular sports volunteering appear to be event and non-sport volunteering. For example, the evidence points to sports-event volunteering increasing for younger volunteers and those previously attending sports events, but with personal development from the Games. Moreover, greater desire to be involved in non-sports events is also enhanced by evidence personal development from the Games. Finally, there is evidence that younger Games volunteers and those with prior experience of volunteering have their interest in non-sports volunteering enhanced. Significantly, as Table 1 reveals, it is these latter aspects of volunteering that appear to be more strongly influenced generally by experience of the Games than all of the other effects.

The policy implications of these findings seem to relatively clear. First, for both those with previous sports and other volunteering experience, volunteering at a major sports event is more likely to raise interest in non-sports volunteering than other potential sports development targets, although there is an effect on the latter. Second, it is for the younger volunteer that most pronounced effects are identified. In this regard investments in events are more likely to have wider social capital returns than enhanced sports development consequences. Third, and probably as a result, personal development appears to be a general 'driver' as far as both sports development and non-sports volunteering development are concerned.

Consequently this research suggests that in order to capitalize upon the sports development implications of volunteering at a major event, organizers need to focus, first of all, on promoting and harnessing the personal development of volunteers. As indicated in Table 2 this suggests ensuring the fulfilment of, and promoting the possibility that through volunteering:

- It improved my chances of employment
- It looks good on my CV and Application forms
- I have learned new skills and capabilities
- I enhanced and developed my skills
- I have enhanced my personal development
- I have increased my self-confidence
- It provided new challenges
- It changed my life.

However, as the research also indicates that non-sports related developments are more likely, then this suggests, second, a strong need to both emphasize and harness the sports development opportunities produced, if this is a policy priority. In essence this means overtly promoting a serious leisure career. It is clear that providing "structural" links between volunteering and, say, subsequent sports participation and volunteering opportunities are needed to communicate and promote the ongoing benefits and status of volunteering.

As discussed in Burgham & Downward (2005), economic and social incentives could be developed and used. For example, collaboration with sport, leisure and event-management examining bodies could be a way in which initial event experience and then enhanced more regular volunteering could be used to formalize the development of transferable skills making CV enhancement tangible, perhaps in the context of "lifelong learning". In the UK, Sport England (2003) argue that this might be an important source of core funding for sports generally, through linkages to Learning and Skills policies being mediated through sports clubs. Likewise, tax incentives could be lobbied for from public authorities, for those who volunteer to reduce the extent of any income–leisure trade-off faced by individuals, which, as noted above, may be present in more regular sports participation and volunteering.[6] By essentially producing payment in kind, this might allow event volunteers to access the patterns of higher income sports participation and sports volunteering that forms the key volunteer segment of the population. This would be of particular relevance to the young through, perhaps, concessions on student loans being offered.

This is important because the above research places emphasis on the potential of younger volunteers. Sport England (2003), moreover, identifies the younger volunteer generally with less formal and systematic involvement in volunteering and, while not lacking interest in sports, needing flexible-time options for getting involved with and experience of volunteering.[7] Importantly tax and loan concessions are specific to the individual and could remain operative without funding sports clubs directly first. In this regard the only extra administrative duty would be some sort of audited record keeping.

It is also important to reiterate at this point, however, that the results above do point to investment in events yielding wider social capital enhancement through non-sports volunteering. This may mitigate against the need for any direct and indirect increase in funding to sports per se if this, in itself, is the desired policy outcome. Moreover, this might be attractive to policy makers particularly as it might be argued that traditional sports participation and volunteering patterns represent relatively closed networks implied in the profiles of volunteers discussed above. It is clear, thus, that the above research raises important issues for public policy choice and emphasis. This is particularly the case for those advocating the need to develop wider sports participation and volunteering profiles.

Conclusions

Most of the literature on evaluating public investment in sports has focused upon the construction or relocation of facilities and the hosting of events and their potential economic benefits to a community; either in tangible or intangible terms. Less is written about the intangible impacts, and, in particular, the human legacy. This research contributes to filling this gap in the literature by exploring the impact on the interest in sport, sports participation, sport and non-sport volunteering that follow from the experience of volunteering at the XVII Manchester Commonwealth Games.

The research reveals that events are complex sports related policy interventions that can change the structures of leisure demands, expressed as participation or volunteering. However, while the research reveals that experience of volunteering at a major event can raise interest, participation and volunteering in sport, this is less likely than promoting interest in wider societal volunteering, that is development of non-sport social capital. Thus, whereas the development impacts generally appear stronger for the younger volunteer, and when personal development is enhanced, the latter of which is clearly suggestive of a focus for volunteer recruitment strategy, nonetheless elements of a policy trade-off between sports and non-sport social capital improvements are evident. Clearly, further longitudinal research is required that explores these transitions to help to critically assess these findings and contribute to public policy debate.

Notes

1. This research was funded by UK Sport. The paper has benefited from feedback from presentations at the European Association of Sports Management Conference in Newcastle upon Tyne, UK, held in September 2005, a seminar to the Faculty of Sport, Health and Exercise at Staffordshire University in November 2005, discussion with colleagues at Loughborough, and comments from Holger Preuss and anonymous referees.
2. The research also investigated volunteer expectations in a questionnaire issued to the same respondents prior to the Games. More detail on the results concerning the expectations of volunteering are available in the papers Ralston *et al.* 2004; Downward and Ralston 2005, and Downward *et al.* 2005. A more general overview of other elements of the research project is obtainable from UK Sport at www.uksport.gov.uk/
3. The dependent variables' scales were thus treated as essentially ordinal rather than interval magnitudes. The factor analysis was conducted on SPSS version 12, and the regression analysis on STATA SE version 8.
4. With the multiple categories implied in the series of nominal variables Age 1 to 4 and Emp 1 to 4, Age1 and Emp1 were excluded from the analysis to avoid the 'dummy variable trap'.
5. While statistical significance is always connected to sample size, comparisons across models on broadly the same number of observations is meaningful. Moreover, in applied research statistics can only have intrinsic meaning in connection to the variables used and implied theoretical motivation for using them.
6. A full set of results for the regressions and factor analysis are available from the author on request.
7. However, as Burgham and Downward (2005) note, this may involve some compromise with a traditional volunteering ethos.

References

Baade, R. (1996). Professional sports as catalysts for metropolitan economic development. *Journal of Urban Affairs*, 18(1), 1–17.

Baade, R. A. (2003). Evaluating subsidies for professional sports in the United States and Europe: A public-sector primer. *Oxford Review of Economic Policy*, 19(4), 585–597.

Baade, R., & Dye, R. (1990). The impact of stadiums and professional sports on metropolitan area development. *Growth and Change*, 20(2), 1–14.

Baade, R. A., & Matheson, V. A. (2004). The quest for the cup: assessing the economic impact of the World Cup. *Regional Studies, 38,* 343 354.

Burgham, M., & Downward, P. M. (2005). Why volunteer, time to volunteer? A case study from swimming. *Managing Leisure, 10*(2), 1–15.

Chalip, L. (2000). Sydney 2000: Volunteers and the organisation of the Olympic Games: Economic and formative aspects. In M. Moragas, A. Moreno, and N. Puig (Eds.), *Symposium on Volunteers, Global Society and the Olympic Movement.* Lausanne 24–26 November, 1999. International Olympic Committee.

Coates, D., & Humphreys, B. R. (1999). The growth effects of sports franchises, stadia and arenas. *Journal of Policy Analysis and Management, 18*(4), 601–624.

Coleman, R. (2002). Characteristics of volunteering in UK sport: Lessons from cricket. *Managing Leisure, 7,* 220–238.

Coyne, B., & Coyne, J. (2001). Getting, keeping and caring for unpaid volunteers at professional golf tournament events. *Human Resource Development International, 4*(2), 199–214.

Crompton, J. (1995). Economic impact analysis of sports facilities and events: Eleven sources of misapplication. *Journal of Sports Management, 9,* 14–35.

Crompton, J. (2004). Beyond economic impact: An alternative rationale for the subsidy of major league sports facilities. *Journal of Sports Management, 18,* 40–58.

Davis-Smith, J. (1998). *The 1997 National Survey of Volunteering.* London: The National Centre for Volunteering.

Downward, P. M. (2004). Assessing neoclassical microeconomic theory via leisure demand: A post Keynesian perspective. *Journal of Post Keynesian Economics, 26*(3), 371–395.

Downward, P. M. (forthcoming). Exploring the economic choice to participate in sport: Results from the 2002 General Household Survey. *The International Review of Applied Economics.*

Downward, P. M., Lumsdon, L., & Ralston, R. (2005). Gender differences in sports event volunteering: Insights from Crew 2002 at the XVII Commonwealth Games. *Managing Leisure: An International Journal, 10,* 219–256.

Downward, P. M., & Ralston, R. (2005). Volunteer motivation and expectations prior to the XVII Commonwealth Games in Manchester, UK. *Tourism and Hospitality Planning and Development, 2*(1), 17–26.

Farrell, J., Johnston, M., & Twynam, G. (1998). Volunteer motivation, satisfaction and management at an elite sporting competition. *Journal of Sport Management, 12,* 288–300.

Gratton, C., Nichols, G., Shibli, S., & Taylor, P. (1997). *Valuing Volunteers in UK Sport.* London: Sports Council.

Gratton, C., Shibli, S., & Coleman, R. (2005). Sport and economic regeneration in cities. *Urban Studies, 42*(5/6), 985–999.

Gratton, C. & Taylor, P. (2000). *The Economics of Sport and Recreation.* London: E & F Spon.

Green, K., Smith, A., & Roberts, K. (2005). Young people and lifelong participation in sport and physical activity: a sociological perspective of contemporary physical education programmes in England and Wales. *Leisure Studies, 24*(1), 27–43.

Hair, J. F., Anderson, R. E., & Tatham, R. L. (1990). *Multivariate Data Analysis.* New York: Macmillan.

Harrington, M., Cuskelly, G., & Auld, C. (2000). Career volunteering in commodity-intensive serious leisure: Motorsport events and their dependence on volunteers/amateurs. *Loisir et Societie/Leisure and Society, 23*(2), 421–452.

Hudson, I. (2001). The use and misuse of economic impact analysis: The case of professional sports. *Journal of Sport and Social Issues, 25*(1), 20–39.

Long, J. S., & Freese, J. (2003). *Regression Models for Categorical Dependent Variables using Stata.* College Station, TX: Stata Press.

MacAloon, J. (2000). Volunteers, global society and the Olympic movement. In M. Moragas, A. Moreno, & N. Puig (Eds.), *Symposium on Volunteers, Global Society and the Olympic Movement.* Lausanne, 24–26 November 1999. International Olympic Committee.

Moreno, A., Moragas, M., & Paniagua, R. (2000). The evolution of volunteers at the Olympic Games. In M. Moragas, A. Moreno & N. Puig (Eds.) *Symposium on Volunteers, Global Society and the Olympic Movement*. Lausanne 24–26 November 1999. International Olympic Committee.

Nichols, G. (2004). Pressures on volunteers in the UK. In R. A. Stebbins, & M. Graham (Eds.), *Volunteering as Leisure/Leisure as Volunteering: An International Assessment*. Wallingford, UK: CABI Publishing.

Nichols, G. (2005). Issues arising from Sport England's survey of volunteers in sport 2002–3. In G. Nichols, & M. Collins (Eds.), *Volunteers in Sports Clubs*. Eastbourne: Leisure Studies Association.

Ralston, R., Downward, P. M., & Lumsdon, L. (2004). The expectations of volunteers prior to the XVII Commonwealth Games, 2002: A qualitative study. *Event Management*, 9, 13–26.

Siegfried, J., & Zimbalist, A. (2000). The economics of sports facilities and their communities. *Journal of Economic Perspectives*, 14(3), 95–14.

Sport England (2003). *Sports Volunteering In England 2002*, Retrieved December 2004, from www.sportengland.org/index/get_resources/resource_downloads/research_and_reports.htm

Stata (2003). *Reference N-R, Volume 3*. College Station, TX: Stata Press.

Stebbins, R. A. (1982). Serious leisure: A conceptual statement. *Pacific Sociological Review*, 25(2), 251–272.

Padding Required: Assessing the Economic Impact of the Super Bowl

VICTOR A. MATHESON* & ROBERT A. BAADE**

*College of the Holy Cross, Worcester, USA, **Lake Forest College, USA*

A joint study conducted by the National Football League (NFL) and the Sport Management Research Institute (SMRI) of Westin, Florida estimated an economic impact of $393 million from Super Bowl XXXIII on the South Florida economy (NFL, 1999b). If those numbers are accurate, "Super" is an apt adjective for the event. Only the Summer Olympic Games can seriously be thought to generate an impact of such magnitude for a short-term sporting event. Reasons for skepticism, however, abound, and one may well need look no further than the NFL's motivation for making such lofty claims. Can a study either commissioned or performed by the NFL be unbiased if the NFL has used the promise of a future Super Bowl as an enticement for cities to build new facilities? Modern sports stadiums generally receive some form of public funding, and the NFL, at least indirectly, has rationalized public financial support on the grounds that the economic impact from a single Super Bowl approximates the cost of building a new stadium. Coincidence? The purpose of this study is to estimate the economic impact of Super Bowls from 1970 through 2001. The results indicate that the economic impact of the Super Bowl is likely on average one-quarter or less the magnitude of the most recent NFL estimates.

Review of Super Bowl Impact Studies

The economic impact estimates for the Super Bowl extend from one intellectual end zone to the other. The NFL-SMRI study is the most optimistic appraisal attributing a $670 million increase in taxable sales in South Florida (Miami-Dade, Broward and Palm Beach counties) and an increase in economic activity of $396 million to the event (NFL, 1999b). Tacitly, the NFL-commissioned study envisioned a horde of affluent spendthrifts descending on the three-county area. The NFL-SMRI team reported that the average income of Super Bowl attendees is more than twice that of the average visitor to South Florida during the peak tourist months of January and February ($144,500 compared to $40,000–$80,000), and they spend up to four times as much as the average visitor to South Florida ($400.33 per day compared to $99–$199 per day). Jim Steeg, the NFL's Vice President for special events from 1977–2005, puts the Super Bowl at the centre of the mega-event universe.

> The Super Bowl is the most unique of all special events. Extensive studies by host cities, independent organizations and the NFL all try to predict the economic impact the big game will have on a community. They talk to tens of thousands of attendees, local businessmen, corporate planners, media and local fans—looking to see how they are affected.
>
> These studies have provided irrefutable evidence that a Super Bowl is the most dramatic event in the US Super Bowl patrons are significantly more affluent, spend more and have more spent on them, and influence future business in the community more than attendees of any other event or convention held in the US. (Steeg, 1999)

Steeg based his Super Bowl claims on several factors. Most prominent among them from his perspective were: the substantial spending by the NFL and NFL Properties;[1] the number of visitors from outside the community who attended the game and related events; and the ideal fit of the Super Bowl into the convention calendar, which Steeg opined has the capacity for transforming the historically slack month of January into a convention windfall for the host city.

The NFL understands that it is competing for the sports entertainment dollar, and the League believes that stadiums factor prominently into consumer decisions relating to leisure spending. With the completion of stadium construction in Chicago, Green Bay and Philadelphia, 21 NFL stadiums will have been built or significantly refurbished over the period 1995 through 2003. This substantial transformation of NFL infrastructure has been accomplished in part through league incentives to include hosting a Super Bowl in some cases and using League shared club seat revenues to help finance stadium construction.[2] In light of the NFL's strategic success, Steeg's claims warrant further scrutiny.

Scholars not directly connected to the NFL disagree on the economic impact of the Super Bowl. In assessing the impact of Super Bowl XXVIII on the City of

Atlanta and the State of Georgia, Jeffrey Humphreys (1994) estimated that the event created 2,736 jobs and had an impact of $166 million on the Georgia economy. Of the $166 million, Humphreys estimated direct and indirect economic impact of $76 and $90 million, respectively. The direct impact was derived from estimating the number of "visitor days" (306,680) and multiplying that statistic by the average estimated per diem expenditures per visitor ($252). The indirect or induced economic impact was estimated using the Regional Input–Output Multiplier System (RIMS II) model developed by the Bureau of Economic Analysis. A portion of the roughly $230 million difference between the estimates for Super Bowls XXXIII and XXVIII is explained by price increases, but most of the difference is attributable to the number of visitors and the daily spending attributable to each of them. In Table 1, a sample of economic impact estimates for selected Super Bowls from 1995 through 2003 are recorded to help provide a context for the impact of the event.

Phil Porter (1999) has provided a far less sanguine appraisal of the Super Bowl's economic impact. Porter used regression analysis to determine that the impact of the event was statistically insignificant, that is not measurably different from zero. After reviewing short-term data[3] on sales receipts for several Super Bowls, Porter concluded:

> Investigator bias, data measurement error, changing production relationships, diminishing returns to both scale and variable inputs, and capacity constraints anywhere along the chain of sales relations lead to lower multipliers. Crowding out and price increases by input suppliers in response to higher levels of demand and the tendency of suppliers to lower prices to stimulate sales when demand is weak lead to overestimates of net new sales due to the event. These characteristics alone would suggest that the estimated impact of the mega-sporting event will be lower than the impact analysis predicts.

Table 1. Economic Impact Estimates Provided by Boosters for Selected Super Bowls Between 1995 and 2003

Year	Author	City	Estimate in millions of $ and (in millions of 2000 $)
1995	NFL and Kathleen Davis, Sports Management Research Institute	Miami	$365 ($412.4)
1998	PriceWaterhouseCoopers	San Diego	$295 ($311.7)
1999	NFL and Kathleen Davis, Sports Management Research Institute	Miami	$393 ($406.2)
2000	Jason Ader, Bear Stearns	Atlanta	$410 ($410)
2000	Jeffrey Humphreys, Georgia State University	Atlanta	$292 ($292)
2003	Super Bowl Host Committee	San Diego	$375 ($356.8)

Similarly, Baade & Matheson's (2000) examination of 25 Super Bowls from 1973 to 1997 found the game associated with an increase in host metropolitan area employment of 537 jobs. Based on simple assumptions regarding the value of a job to a community, they estimate an average economic impact of roughly $30 million or roughly one-tenth the figures touted by the NFL. Coates & Humphrey's (2002) look at all post-season play in American professional sports found that hosting the Super Bowl had no statistically significant effect on per capita income in the host city.

From 1995 through 2003, approximately $6.4 billion dollars, or an average of $304 million, will have been spent to build or substantially refurbish 21 NFL stadiums. The public contribution will have been $4.4 billion, an average of $209 million, or roughly 69% of the construction costs of these facilities (Peter, 2002). The NFL has offered the Super Bowl as an inducement to convince otherwise reluctant cities that the construction of a new stadium makes economic sense. (It's hard to believe that the NFL would choose to place the Super Bowl in Detroit in January of 2006 except for the presence of the newly constructed Ford Field.) Scholars do not agree on the economic impact of the Super Bowl, and in the next section of the paper, reasons for the disagreement are identified and analysed.

Theoretical Issues

If there is an exaggeration of the benefits induced by a sports mega-event, it occurs for several fundamental reasons. First, the increase in direct spending attributable to the games may be a "gross" as opposed to a "net" measure. Some subsidy advocates estimate direct spending by simply summing all receipts associated with the event. The fact that the gross-spending approach fails to account for decreased spending directly attributable to the event represents a major theoretical and practical shortcoming. Surveys on expenditures by those attending the event, complete with a question on place of residence, would appear to be a straightforward way of estimating direct expenditures in a manner that is statistically acceptable. However, while such surveys may well provide acceptable spending estimates for those patronizing the event, they do not reveal changes in spending by residents not attending it. It is conceivable that some local residents or potential visitors may dramatically change their spending given their desire to avoid the congestion at least in the venue's environs. A basic shortcoming of typical economic impact studies, in general, pertains not to information on spending by those included in a direct expenditure survey, but rather to the lack of information on the spending behaviour for those who are not.

Robert Baade (1996) has cited the failure to account for the difference between gross and net spending as a chief reason why sports events or teams do not contribute as much to metropolitan economies as boosters claim. However, in the case of a "mega-event", a large proportion of all attendees come from outside the local area, and their spending qualifies as export spending. If the host city's residents who do not attend do not reduce their expenditures within the city, one might contend that direct expenditure by nonresidents who attend events approximates net impact. Unfortunately, this will not be true if some nonresidents, who might have visited the city, decide not to do so because of congestion and high prices during the event's period. In addition, some Super Bowl fans may have already been planning on visiting a city but rearrange their schedule to accommodate the sporting event. Even though the economic analyst may attribute this visit to the athletic contest, in fact this type of time switching does not lead to a net increase in economic activity in the city but simply alters the time period in which the activity takes place.

Recent evidence assessing the economic impact of the Summer Olympics in 2000 in Sydney, Australia indicate this particular "substitution effect" may be substantial even in cases where the event has a clear international character. An Arthur Andersen (2000) survey on hotel activity in Sydney and other capital cities prior to and during the Olympic Games concluded:

> As expected, survey results indicate the vast majority of Sydney hotels peaking at near 100% occupancies during the Games period from September 16–30. This represents an increase of 49% in occupancy levels relative to the first half of September. In contrast, other capital cities experienced significant demand shortfalls for the same period. For example, occupancies in Melbourne and Brisbane plummeted by 19% and 17% in the second half of September relative to the period from 1–15 September. Overall, with the exception of Sydney and Adelaide, all hotel markets in Australia experienced a decline in occupancy in September 2000 relative to September 1999 despite the Olympic Games, as reported in the Hotel Industry Benchmark Survey. Hoteliers indicate that while international demand was strong ..., domestic leisure travel traditionally taking place during the September school holiday period was displaced to Sydney for the Olympics.

The Anderson report indicates the importance of the substitution effect, and compels consideration of which, if any, governmental entities should be involved in subsidizing sports mega-events. Sydney's gains may well have come at the expense of other Australian cities, and if the federal government subsidizes the games there must be a rationale for enriching Sydney at the expense of Adelaide and other regional cities.

A second reason economic impact may be exaggerated relates to what economists refer to as the "multiplier", the notion that direct spending increases induce additional rounds of spending due to increased incomes that occur as a result of additional spending.[4] If errors are made in assessing direct spending, those errors are compounded in calculating indirect spending through standard multiplier analysis. Furthermore, correct multiplier analysis includes all "leakages" from the circular flow of payments and uses multipliers that are appropriate to the event industry. Leakages may be significant depending on the state of the economy. If the host economy is at or very near full employment, for example, it may be that the labour essential to conducting the event resides in other communities where unemployment or a labour surplus exists. To the extent that this is true, then the indirect spending that constitutes the multiplier effect must be adjusted to reflect this leakage of income and subsequent spending. Siegfried & Zimbalist (2002) note that only 29% of professional athletes in their study live in the metropolitan area in which their team plays, leading to very high levels of leakage from local expenditures on professional sports. Labour is not the only factor of production that may repatriate income. If hotels experience higher than normal occupancy rates during a mega-event, then the question must be raised about the fraction of increased earnings that remain in the community if the hotel is a nationally owned chain.

Finally, most economic impact analyses use expenditure multipliers (rather than income multipliers) to assess the economic impact of an event. The use of expenditure multipliers is unjustified, however, as the important point is not how much business activity is created by an event but rather how the income of local residents is impacted by it. In short, to assess the impact of mega-events, a balance of payments approach should be utilized. That is to say, to what extent does the event give rise to income inflows and outflows that would not occur in its absence? Since the input–output models used in the most sophisticated *ex-ante* analyses are based on fixed relationships between inputs and outputs, such models do not account for the subtleties of full employment and capital ownership noted here. In addition, these multipliers are based upon inter-industry relationships within regions based upon an economic area's normal production patterns. During mega-events, however, the economy within a region may be anything but normal, and therefore, these same inter-industry relationships may not hold. Indeed, since the benefits may largely accrue to non-local labour and capital owners leading to higher than normal leakages of income, the money generated from these events is unlikely to recirculate through the economy (Matheson, 2004). Normal multipliers are therefore probably inflated.

As an alternative to estimating the change in expenditures and associated changes in economic activity, those who provide goods and services directly in accommodating the event could be asked how their activity has been altered by the event. In summarizing the efficacy of this technique Davidson (1999) opined:

> The biggest problem with this producer approach is that these business managers must be able to estimate how much "extra" spending was caused by the sport event. This requires that each proprietor have a model of what would have happened during that time period had the sport event not taken place. This is an extreme requirement, which severely limits this technique.

While the focus of this paper is on the estimated benefits of the Super Bowl, the cost side of the equation should not be ignored. Most league-sponsored economic impact studies not only potentially inflate the benefit-side of the cost–benefit equation but also generally completely ignore the costs of hosting such an event. Besides the infrastructure costs associated with hosting the game, the variable costs borne by the city in terms of added police, fire and sanitation services are at least $1.5 million for the Super Bowl (Coates & Humphreys, 2006) and exceeded $1.5 billion for the multi-day, multi-venue Athens Olympics in 2004.

Of course, one solution to the criticisms of *ex-ante* economic analysis is to simply perform better cost–benefit analysis that more thoroughly addresses the issues of appropriate multipliers, opportunity costs and the substitution effects of the Super Bowl. Given the practical difficulties involved with this approach, however, this paper instead looks back at the experiences of host cities to examine whether the advertised *ex-ante* estimates conform to *ex-post* estimates of the economic impact this event exerts on its host cities. In the next section of the paper, the model that is used to develop *ex-post* estimates is detailed.

The Model

Ex- ante models may not provide credible estimates on the economic impact of a mega-event for the reasons cited. An *ex-post* model may be useful in providing a filter through which the promises made by event boosters can be strained. A mega-event's impact is likely to be small relative to the overall economy, and the primary challenge for those doing a post-event audit involves isolating the event's impact. This is not a trivial task, and those who seek insight into the question of economic impact should be cognizant of the challenges and deficiencies common to both *ex-ante* and *ex-post* analyses.

Several approaches are possible in constructing a model to estimate the impact an event has had on a city, and are suggested by past scholarly work. Mills & McDonald (1992) provide an extensive summary of models that have been used to explain metropolitan economic growth. These theories seek to explain increases in economic activity through changes in key economic variables in the short run (export base and neoclassical models) or the identification of long-term developments that enhance the capacity for growth in metropolitan economies (product cycle, cumulative causation and disequilibrium dynamic adjustment models).

Our task is not to replicate explanations of metropolitan economic growth, but to use past work to help identify how much of an increase in economic activity in US cities hosting the Super Bowl is attributable to the event. To this end we have selected explanatory variables from existing models to predict economic activity in the absence of the game. Estimating the economic impact of the Super Bowl involves comparing the projected level of economic activity without the event to the actual levels of economic activity that occurred in cities that have hosted it. The success of this approach depends on our ability to identify variables that account for the variation in growth in economic activity in host cities.

Given the number and variety of variables found in regional growth models and the inconsistency of findings with regard to coefficient size and significance, criticisms of any single model could logically focus on the problems posed by omitted variables. Any critic, of course, can claim that a particular regression suffers from omitted-variable bias, but it is far more challenging to specify the model so as to remedy the problem. In explaining regional or metropolitan growth patterns, at least some of the omitted variable problem can be addressed through a careful specification of the independent variables. As noted above, representing relevant variables as deviations from city norms, leaves the scholar a more manageable task, namely that of identifying those factors that explain city growth after accounting for the impact of those forces that generally have affected regional or national metropolitan statistical area (MSA) growth. It is important, for example, to model the fact that relocating a business could occur as a consequence of wages increasing in the MSA under study or a slower rate of wage growth in other MSAs. What matters is not the absolute level of wages in city i, but city i's wage relative to that of its competitors.

The purpose of *ex-ante* studies is to provide a measure of the net benefits a project or event is likely to yield. To our knowledge there is no prospective model that has the capacity for measuring the net benefits of a project relative to the next best alternative use of those funds. If one assumes that the best use of funds has always occurred prior to a mega-event, then the growth path observed for a city can be construed as optimal. If this optimal growth path, identified by the city's secular growth trend, decreases after the mega-event occurs, then the evidence does not support the hypothesis that a publicly subsidized mega-event put those public monies to the best use.

Our model is designed to predict changes in income attributable to the Super Bowl in host cities 1970 and 2001. The cohort of cities used in the sample includes 73 metropolitan areas that represent the largest MSAs in the United States by population over the time period 1970–2001 including every MSA that was among the largest 60 MSAs at some time during that period. While the choice of 73 cities is largely arbitrary, the list was expanded to include all metropolitan areas that have hosted the Super Bowl, cities with professional sports franchises (with the exception of Green Bay, WI), and MSAs with professional sports aspirations. A fuller description of the data is available from the authors upon request.

At this point the analysis can be conducted in two ways. Traditionally, researchers such as Coates & Humphreys (2002) and Baade & Matheson (2000) have used fixed-effect models on this type of panel data with a dummy variable included for the sporting event(s) and individual dummy variables included for each city in the model to account for regional difference in economic growth. Equation (1) represents the model used to predict changes in income for host cities.

$$\Delta Y^i_t = \beta_0 + \beta_1 \Delta Y^i_{t-1} + \beta_2 \frac{Y^i_{t-1}}{\sum_{i=1}^{n} Y^i_{t-1}/n} + \beta_3 W^i_t + \beta_4 G^i_t + \beta_5 OT^i_t$$

$$+ \beta_6 POP^i_t + \beta_7 SB^i_t + \alpha_i C^i + \gamma_i t^i_t + \varepsilon^i_t \tag{1}$$

For each time period t, Y^i_t is the real personal income and ΔY^i_t is the change in real personal income in the ith MSA, n is the number of cities in the sample, W^i_t is the nominal wages in the ith MSA as a percentage of the average for all cities in the sample, G^i_t is the state and local taxes in the ith MSA as a percentage of the average for all cities in the sample, POP^i_t is the log population of the ith city, SB^i_t is a dummy variable for hosting the Super Bowl, and ε^i_t is the stochastic error. OT^i_t is a dummy variable that represents any significant city-specific economic influences that cannot be explained by other variables in the model including the effects of the oil booms of the 1970s and the subsequent oil bust of the 1980s on oil patch cities such as New Orleans and Houston, the effects of Hurricane Andrew on the economy of South Florida, and the economic consequences of the tech boom in Silicon Valley. C^i is a vector of dummy variables representing the fixed effect for each city i, and t is a vector of dummy variables representing each year t representing the business cycle. By specifying variables that either represent wages or taxes a percentage of the average, and by using lagged income percentages, problems of endogeneity are largely avoided.

The results of ordinary least-squares regression using equation (1) are shown in Table 2. The coefficient (0.4058%) and t-statistic (1.409) on the Super Bowl variable indicate that hosting the Super Bowl is associated with an increase in city personal income growth of 0.4% but that this figure is not statistically significantly different from zero at a 10% level. Thus, little confidence can be placed in any claim that the Super Bowl results in positive economic benefits for the host city.

While the use of fixed-effect models is widespread due to their simplicity, they present numerous theoretical and applied difficulties that make their use undesirable when they can be avoided. First, the assumptions implicit in the model are quite extreme in that it is assumed the only difference in city growth rates is a fixed percentage in each period. This belies the fact that some cities (such as Detroit or San Jose) are strongly influenced by cyclical industries, and others have experienced growth spurts or slowdowns at varying times in their recent history. To assume that every economic variable affects every city's economic growth in exactly the same way is an absurd albeit often necessary assumption. Next heteroscedasticity is identified as a problem since the variability of the residuals differs widely between cities. For example, the standard deviation of the residuals for the data representing Minneapolis is 0.0056 while the standard deviation of San Jose's residuals is 0.0220, and a Goldfield–Quandt test for equality of residual variance can be rejected at well beyond a 1% significance level.

In addition, because the size of the economies of the host cities varies widely, it is difficult to translate the coefficient indicating a 0.4% increase in

Table 2. Regression Results for Fixed Effect Model

Model fit

R-square	Adjusted R-square	Standard error of the estimate	Durbin–Watson
0.7644	0.7509	0.01474	2.03963

Coefficients (dependent variable = %Δ Income)

Independent variables	Coefficients			
	B	Std. Error	t-stat	Significance
(Constant)	0.3827	0.0493	7.764	0.0000
%Δ Income (t − 1)	0.4432	0.0207	21.366	0.0000
Log population	−0.0519	0.0074	−7.006	0.0000
Income as% of sample average (t − 1)	−0.0343	0.0077	−4.452	0.0000
Taxes as% of sample average	−0.0018	0.006	−0.291	0.7714
Wages as% of sample average (t − 1)	−0.0335	0.0078	−4.287	0.0000
Hurricane Andrew	−0.0399	0.0107	−3.736	0.0002
Hurricane Andrew recovery	0.0582	0.0088	6.607	0.0000
Tech Boom 1	0.0478	0.0089	5.370	0.0000
Tech Boom 2	0.0804	0.0090	8.937	0.0000
Tech Bust	−0.0978	0.0093	−10.497	0.0000
Super Bowl	**0.0041**	**0.0029**	**1.409**	**0.1590**
Oil Boom 1	0.0099	0.0040	2.505	0.0123
Oil Boom 2	0.0153	0.0035	4.400	0.0000
Oil Bust	−0.0268	0.0032	−8.483	0.0000
Albany–Schenectady–Troy (MSA)	−0.0067	0.0054	−1.243	0.2141
...				
Year 2001	−0.0112	0.0025	−4.479	0.0000
...				

Note: Fixed effects for individual cities/years shown for Albany MSA and the year 2001 but are excluded for remaining years and cities. Full results are available from the authors upon request.

economic growth into a convenient dollar figure. Indeed, if the Super Bowl is, say, a $400 million event, there is no reason to think that economic growth in each city would be altered by the same amount since percentage-wise such an impact would be different in a small city such as New Orleans compared to a large city such as Los Angeles. Finally, a confidence interval for the Super Bowl variable ranges from a negative range to roughly a 1% gain in city income, which would correspond to roughly an $800 million income in city income for the average host city. So, while a hypothesis of no income gain from hosting the Super Bowl cannot be rejected, nor can the booster's predictions of a $400 million gain be rejected.

While some of these issues, as well as potential serial correlation problems, can be dealt with a more advance time-series, panel data regression model, we instead propose a wholly different approach. Equation (2) represents the revised model used to predict changes in income for host cities.

$$\Delta Y_t^i = \beta_0 + \beta_1 \sum_{i=1}^{n} \frac{\Delta Y_t^i}{n_t} + \beta_2\, \Delta Y_{t-1}^i + \beta_3\, \frac{Y_{t-1}^i}{\sum_{i=1}^{n} Y_{t-1}^i / n} + \beta_4 W_t^i + \beta_5\, T_t^i$$

$$+ \beta_6\, TR_t^i + \beta_7\, OT_t^i + \alpha SB_t^i + \varepsilon_t^i \qquad (2)$$

The variables remain the same as in equation (1) except for the Super Bowl variable. SB_t^i is now a vector of dummy variables representing the Super Bowl with a separate dummy variable being included for each year a particular city has hosted the game. The major change is that equation (2) was separately estimated for each of the 11 different metropolitan areas that have hosted at least one Super Bowl since 1970 instead of as a panel. Not every variable specified in equation (2) emerged as statistically significant for every city. The decision of whether to include an independent variable known to be a good predictor in general but failing to be statistically significant in a particular city's case is largely an arbitrary one. The inclusion of theoretically valuable variables that are idiosyncratically insignificant will improve some measures of fit such as R-squared but may reduce other measures such as adjusted R-squared or the standard error of the estimate. Since the purpose of equation (2) is to produce predictive rather than explanatory results, variables were included in the regression equation as long as they improved predictive success, and as long as the omission of the variable did not significantly alter the coefficients of the remaining variables. Table 3 presents the regression results for all cities with the combination of variables that minimizes the standard error of the estimate (SEE). Note that Table 3 does not report the regression results for the Super Bowl dummy variables, which are instead reported in Table 4. Finally, Durbin-Watson statistics were calculated for each of the eleven regression equations in Table 3. The results of the Durbin–Watson statistics suggested that serial correlation was not a significant problem in any of the eleven regression equations.

As mentioned previously, rather than specifying all the variables that may explain metropolitan growth, we attempted to simplify the task by including only the independent variables that are common to cities in general and the ith MSA in particular. In effect we have devised a structure that attempts to identify the extent to which the deviations from the growth of cities in general ($\Sigma \Delta Y_t^i / n_t$) and city i's secular growth ΔY_{t-1}^i, are attributable to deviations in certain costs of production (wages and taxes) or demand-side variables (relative income levels, wages, and taxes).

Relative values of wages and tax burdens are all expected to help explain a city's growth rate in income as it deviates from the sample norm and its own secular growth path. As mentioned above, past research has not produced consistency with respect to the signs and significance of these independent variables. It is not at all clear, for example, whether high levels of relative wages lead to higher or lower income growth. A similar situation exists with relative levels of taxation. As a consequence, *a-priori* expectations are

Table 3. Regression Results for Equation (2) (t-stats in Parentheses). Coefficients for Super Bowl Dummy Variables are Omitted from Results and Instead Shown in Table 4

MSA	Cons.	Average Y_t	Y_{t-1}	Y_{t-2}	Y_{t-3}	Income as %	Wages as %	Taxes as %	Log population	Time	Other	Fit
Atlanta	−15.85 (−3.30)	1.092 (8.02)	.232 (2.44)	.090 (0.92)	.034 (034)	−.616 (−2.74)	—	−.395 (−2.93)	−.698 (−2.61)	.0107 (3.124)	—	Adj. R^2 = .9027 SEE = 0.9729%
Detroit	.024 (3.79)	1.166 (8.21)	.432 (5.17)	—	—	−.815 (−4.76)	−.107 (−0.70)	−.164 (−1.61)	1.354 (2.86)	−.004 (−3.31)	—	Adj. R^2 = .9314 SEE = 0.9314%
Houston	.192 (2.37)	.737 (3.13)	.395 (2.35)	—	—	−.185 (−2.27)	—	—	—	—	.0402 (2.84) −.0416 (−2.66)	Adj. R^2 = .5186 SEE = 2.3443%
Los Angeles	−1.902 (−1.69)	.968 (7.37)	.218 (2.11)	—	—	—	—	—	−.621 (−1.92)	.0031 (1.90)	—	Adj. R^2 = .7308 SEE = 1.3386%
Miami	12.14 (2.42)	.904 (5.92)	.260 (2.14)	—	—	−.671 (−2.35)	.430 (2.32)	—	—	−.006 (−2.45)	−.0805 (−5.11) .0865 (3.47)	Adj. R^2 = .8461 SEE = 1.4108%
Mpls.	−.869 (−3.64)	1.042 (18.12)	.058 (1.12)	—	—	−.269 (−2.70)	.212 (2.25)	—	.144 (4.22)	—	—	Adj. R^2 = .9521 SEE = 0.5115%
New Orleans	.320 (2.52)	.601 (3.78)	—	—	—	−.179 (−1.96)	—	−.191 (−2.51)	—	.0153 (1.79)	−.0213 (−2.33)	Adj. R^2 = .5768 SEE = 1.3397%
Phoenix	−33.19 (−2.10)	1.310 (8.50)	.516 (5.942)	.327 (2.86)	—	−1.104 (−3.39)	.427 (3.11)	−.187 (−2.54)	−1.597 (2.71)	.0221 (2.27)	—	Adj. R^2 = .8635 SEE = 1.3188%

Table 3 (*Continued*)

MSA	Cons.	Average Y_t	Y_{t-1}	Y_{t-2}	Y_{t-3}	Income as %	Wages as %	Taxes as %	Log population	Time	Other	Fit
San Diego	1.036 (3.37)	1.023 (8.56)	.240 (2.87)	—	—	—	-.227 (-2.69)	—	-.127 (-3.39)	—	—	Adj. R^2 = .8360 SEE = 1.1329%
San Jose	-11.54 (-4.72)	1.138 (8.22)	—	-.	—	-.362 (-7.09)	-.643 (-4.68)	.150 (2.25)	—	.0063 (4.88)	.0900 (5.44) .1815 (10.46)	Adj. R^2 = .8919 SEE = 1.5260%
Tampa	-9.215 (-1.78)	0.909 (5.44)	.311 (2.64)	—	—	-.529 (-1.68)	-.309 (-1.97)	-.392 (-2.00)	-.815 (-1.96)	.0077 (1.94)	—	Adj. R^2 = .7303 SEE = 1.3746%

Table 4. Super Bowl Contribution to Local Economies

Year	City	Real income (2000 $)	Pred. growth	Actual growth	Difference (S.B. coeff.)	t-stat	Income +/−
1970	New Orleans	$ 18,748,279	1.776%	1.860%	0.084%	0.061	$ 15,796
1971	Miami	$ 27,239,344	7.182%	5.332%	−1.850%	−1.020	$ (503,947)
1972	New Orleans	$ 20,493,238	4.281%	5.855%	1.574%	1.052	$ 322,620
1973	Los Angeles	$ 166,013,025	4.911%	1.941%	−2.970%	−2.006	$ (4,929,805)
1974	Houston	$ 47,263,119	8.079%	7.471%	−0.608%	−0.221	$ (287,386)
1975	New Orleans	$ 22,191,318	2.549%	2.447%	−0.102%	−0.066	$ (22,664)
1976	Miami	$ 31,966,339	3.434%	2.083%	−1.351%	−0.746	$ (431,897)
1977	Los Angeles	$ 178,631,079	4.810%	3.983%	−0.827%	−0.558	$ (1,477,256)
1978	New Orleans	$ 26,342,160	3.520%	5.852%	2.332%	1.609	$ 614,179
1979	Miami	$ 35,677,084	2.890%	2.567%	−0.323%	−0.210	$ (115,390)
1980	Los Angeles	$ 190,215,123	−0.688%	−1.584%	−0.896%	−0.602	$ (1,704,380)
1981	New Orleans	$ 28,341,623	2.316%	4.089%	1.773%	1.159	$ 502,444
1982	Detroit	$ 95,268,030	−2.905%	−4.366%	−1.462%	−1.282	$ (1,392,485)
1983	Los Angeles	$ 198,917,705	2.600%	3.414%	0.814%	0.585	$ 1,618,840
1984	Tampa	$ 40,867,873	7.323%	7.707%	0.383%	0.219	$ 156,553
1985	San Jose	$ 46,226,956	4.311%	3.069%	−1.242%	−0.762	$ (574,343)
1986	New Orleans	$ 29,492,582	−0.311%	−1.166%	−0.855%	−0.550	$ (252,203)
1987	Los Angeles	$ 240,763,733	2.230%	4.440%	2.210%	1.523	$ 5,321,99³
1988	San Diego	$ 66,440,307	4.189%	5.394%	1.206%	0.990	$ 800,941
1989	Miami	$ 47,494,929	1.868%	4.078%	2.210%	1.497	$ 1,049,803
1990	New Orleans	$ 29,669,092	1.247%	1.600%	0.353%	0.244	$ 104,677
1991	Tampa	$ 51,242,892	−0.896%	−1.330%	−0.434%	−0.270	$ (222,309)
1992	Minneapolis	$ 79,702,545	3.413%	4.050%	0.637%	1.101	$ 508,062
1993	Los Angeles	$ 243,170,360	−0.256%	−2.506%	−2.250%	−1.583	$ (5,471,429)
1994	Atlanta	$ 96,197,361	4.644%	5.381%	0.737%	0.624	$ 709,310
1995	Miami	$ 50,355,627	0.344%	3.139%	2.795%	1.792	$ 1,407,511
1996	Phoenix	$ 71,299,199	5.070%	5.598%	0.528%	0.340	$ 376,529
1997	New Orleans	$ 33,755,733	2.137%	2.768%	0.631%	0.450	$ 213,078

Table 4 (*Continued*)

Year	City	Real income (2000 $)	Pred. growth	Actual growth	Difference (S.B. coeff.)	t-stat	Income +/−
1998	San Diego	$ 82,567,615	6.479%	8.457%	1.977%	1.601	$ 1,632,475
1999	Miami	$ 57,068,632	1.458%	3.525%	2.068%	1.321	$ 1,179,931
2000	Atlanta	$ 139,018,879	7.578%	6.368%	−1.210%	−0.968	$ (1,681,953)
2001	Tampa	$ 69,855,497	3.551%	1.066%	−2.485%	−1.093	$ (1,736,037)
	Average		3.098%	3.206%	0.108%	0.132	$ (133,398)

uncertain with regard to the signs of the coefficients. That should not be construed as an absence of theory about key economic relationships. As noted earlier, the models include those variables that previous scholarly work found important.

Results

The coefficients on the dummy variables for the Super Bowl vector for each model identified in Table 3 are an estimate of the effect of the Super Bowl in each specific year on the host city. These coefficients and their corresponding t-stats are shown in Table 4 in the columns labelled "Difference" and "t-stat" along with the real income of each city during the Super Bowl year and the actual observed growth in real income. A predicted personal income growth rate absent the Super Bowl can be calculated by taking the observed growth rate and subtracting out the Super Bowl coefficient. If it is assumed that any difference between actual and predicted income can be accounted for by the presence of the Super Bowl, this method allows for a dollar estimate of the impact of the game on host cities.

For example, the actual personal income growth rate for Phoenix in 1996 was 5.598% while the coefficient on the 1996 Super Bowl dummy variable was 0.528% implying a predicted growth rate absent the Super Bowl of only 5.070% since the model residual for 1996 was 0.000. Based on Phoenix's $71.3 billion economy, this 0.528% difference corresponds to an economy that produced income $377 million in excess of what would have expected during 1996 if the city had not hosted the championship. The $377 million can be interpreted as the contribution of the Super Bowl to the Phoenix economy. In total, the model estimates that the average host city experienced a *reduction* in personal income of $133.4 million relative to the predictions of the model.

The statistics recorded in Table 4 suggest two things worth noting. First, the dollar differences recorded in final column vary substantially with some cities exhibiting income gains well in excess of reasonable booster predictions, and other cities showing a large negative impact. Second, the Super Bowl has an overall negative impact on the host city economy of $133.4 million although this figure is biased downward due to the poor economic performance of Los Angeles in several years. As previously noted, one should resist the temptation to place too much confidence on figures derives from statistically insignificant coefficients; nevertheless, this estimate stands in stark contrast to the annual gains of $300 or $400 million projected by the NFL.

The magnitude of the variation of the estimates at first blush appears high. Some host cities (Los Angeles, 1987 and San Diego, 1998) exhibited well over a billion dollars in increased income while others (Los Angeles, 1993 and 1973, and Atlanta, 2000) experienced reductions of billions of dollars. The explanation for this range of estimates is simply that the models do not explain all the variation in estimated income and, therefore, not all the variation can be attributed to the Super Bowl. In short, there are omitted variables. While the model fit statistics for the individual city regressions display moderately high R-squared numbers, the standard error of the estimate for the typical city is above one percent meaning that one would expected the models to predict actual economic growth for the cities in question within one percentage point less than about two-thirds of the time. For the cities in question, a one percent error translates into a $200 to $500 million difference for the smallest cities such as Miami and New Orleans and over a $2 billion difference for Los Angeles, the largest host city. Given the size of these large, diverse economies, the effect of even a large event with hundreds of millions of dollars of potential impact is likely to be obscured by natural, unexplained variations in the economy. Indeed, none of the standardized residuals are statistically significant at the 5% level.

While it is unlikely that the models for any individual city will capture the effects of even a large event, one would expect that across a large number of cities and years, any event that produces a large impact would emerge on average as statistically significant. The *t*-statistics of the Super Bowl coefficients for the 32 years are normally distributed with a standard deviation of 1. A test on the null hypothesis that the average t-statistic is greater than zero provides a p-value of 23.0%. In other words, if the game really had no positive effect on the host cities, then the sample results had only a 23.0% probability of occurring.

This procedure can be carried one step further. Since the presence of the Super Bowl is not included in making predictions about the economic growth in a particular city, if the Super Bowl has a substantial positive effect on host economies as the boosters suggest, then the appropriate hypothesis test would not be whether the average standardized residual is greater than zero (meaning simply that the event had a positive economic impact) but whether the average standardized residual is greater than some figure that essentially represents a combination of the size of projected impact in comparison to the size of the host city (meaning that the event had a positive economic impact of some designated magnitude).

Table 5 records various estimates that combine estimates provided by NFL boosters and those predicted by the model. For the purpose of exposition, a $300 million Super Bowl (in 2000 dollars) effect is assumed, a figure on the low end of the most recent booster estimates. The model indicates that Phoenix exhibited an increase in income of $377 million over that predicted for the city during 1969 if it had not hosted the game. The difference of $77 million represents the contribution of the Super Bowl to the Phoenix economy above that of boosters' estimates. While the model predicts that Phoenix should have grown 5.070% in 1999 compared with 5.598% actual growth, if a booster estimate of $300 million is accurate and the model's predictors are uncorrelated to the presence of the Super Bowl, the prediction for Phoenix's economic growth would have been 5.491%. Using these new predicted growth rates that include booster growth projections, new t-statistics can be calculated. A new test on the null hypothesis that the new average *t*-statistic is greater than zero provides a p-value of 5.00%. In other words, had the game had a positive effect of $300

Table 5. Super Bowl Contribution to Local Economies assuming a $300 million Super Bowl Boost

Year	City	Income	Super Bowl growth	Model pred. growth	Total pred. growth	Actual growth	Difference	t-stat
1970	New Orleans	$ 18,748,279	1.600%	1.776%	3.376%	1.860%	−1.516%	−1.096
1971	Miami	$ 27,239,344	1.101%	7.182%	8.283%	5.332%	−2.951%	−1.627
1972	New Orleans	$ 20,493,238	1.464%	4.281%	5.745%	5.855%	0.110%	0.074
1973	Los Angeles	$ 166,013,025	0.181%	4.911%	5.092%	1.941%	−3.150%	−2.128
1974	Houston	$ 47,263,119	0.635%	8.079%	8.713%	7.471%	−1.243%	−0.451
1975	New Orleans	$ 22,191,318	1.352%	2.549%	3.901%	2.447%	−1.454%	−0.937
1976	Miami	$ 31,966,339	0.938%	3.434%	4.372%	2.083%	−2.290%	−1.264
1977	Los Angeles	$ 178,631,079	0.168%	4.810%	4.978%	3.983%	−0.995%	−0.671
1978	New Orleans	$ 26,342,160	1.139%	3.520%	4.659%	5.852%	1.193%	0.823
1979	Miami	$ 35,677,084	0.841%	2.890%	3.731%	2.567%	−1.164%	−0.757
1980	Los Angeles	$ 190,215,123	0.158%	−0.688%	−0.531%	−1.584%	−1.054%	−0.708
1981	New Orleans	$ 28,341,623	1.059%	2.316%	3.374%	4.089%	0.714%	0.467
1982	Detroit	$ 95,268,030	0.315%	−2.905%	−2.590%	−4.366%	−1.777%	−1.558
1983	Los Angeles	$ 198,917,705	0.151%	2.600%	2.751%	3.414%	0.663%	0.477
1984	Tampa	$ 40,867,873	0.734%	7.323%	8.058%	7.707%	−0.351%	−0.201
1985	San Jose	$ 46,226,956	0.649%	4.311%	4.960%	3.069%	−1.891%	−1.160
1986	New Orleans	$ 29,492,582	1.017%	−0.311%	0.707%	−1.166%	−1.872%	−1.205
1987	Los Angeles	$ 240,763,733	0.125%	2.230%	2.355%	4.440%	2.086%	1.437
1988	San Diego	$ 66,440,307	0.452%	4.189%	4.640%	5.394%	0.754%	0.619
1989	Miami	$ 47,494,929	0.632%	1.868%	2.499%	4.078%	1.579%	1.069
1990	New Orleans	$ 29,669,092	1.011%	1.247%	2.258%	1.600%	−0.658%	−0.455
1991	Tampa	$ 51,242,892	0.585%	−0.896%	−0.311%	−1.330%	−1.019%	−0.634
1992	Minneapolis	$ 79,702,545	0.376%	3.413%	3.789%	4.050%	0.261%	0.451
1993	Los Angeles	$ 243,170,360	0.123%	−0.256%	−0.132%	−2.506%	−2.373%	−1.670
1994	Atlanta	$ 96,197,361	0.312%	4.644%	4.955%	5.381%	0.425%	0.360
1995	Miami	$ 50,355,627	0.596%	0.344%	0.939%	3.139%	2.199%	1.410
1996	Phoenix	$ 71,299,199	0.421%	5.070%	5.491%	5.598%	0.107%	0.069
1997	New Orleans	$ 33,755,733	0.889%	2.137%	3.026%	2.768%	−0.258%	−0.183

Table 5 (*Continued*)

Year	City	Income	Super Bowl growth	Model pred. growth	Total pred. growth	Actual growth	Difference	t-stat
1998	San Diego	$ 82,567,615	0.363%	6.479%	6.843%	8.457%	1.614%	1.306
1999	Miami	$ 57,068,632	0.526%	1.458%	1.983%	3.525%	1.542%	0.985
2000	Atlanta	$ 139,018,879	0.216%	7.578%	7.794%	6.368%	−1.426%	−1.140
2001	Tampa	$ 69,855,497	0.429%	3.551%	3.980%	1.066%	−2.915%	−1.282
	Average		0.642%	3.098%	3.740%	3.206%	−0.535%	−0.299

million as asserted by the boosters over the thirty-two year period covered by the data, the actual growth rates experienced by the sample would have had only a 5.00% probability of occurring.

The Super Bowl contribution to predicted growth (and hence the standardized residual) can be adjusted by assuming an economic impact larger or smaller than the $300 million figure used in this example. The resulting p-values shown are shown in Table 6.

The predicted economic impact at which the mean t-statistic is zero is $91.9 million, a figure roughly one-quarter that of the booster's estimates, and increases in income of $300.0 million and $392.8 million can be rejected at the 5% and 1% significance levels, respectively. The crowding-out, substitution, and leakages effects can explain the large discrepancy between the observed and actual economic growth and the NFL's claims. While the Super Bowl undoubtedly attracts large numbers of wealthy, out-of-town visitors, the "crowding-out" effect due to perceptions relating to limited hotel rooms and high hotel prices, rowdy behaviour of football fans, and peak use of public goods such as highways and sidewalks are substantial. Furthermore, the net effect on the host economy of the conventions or other tourists who went elsewhere would depend on the details relating to the spending patterns of football fans versus those of the lost visitors and convention attendees. The spending of residents of the host city may be altered to the detriment of the city's economy as local citizens may not frequent areas in which the event occurs or the fans stay. In addition, although hotel room rates in host cities invariably increase substantially during the Super Bowl weekend, to the extent that these hotels are nationally owned chains, the higher prices benefit corporate stockholders, not local residents and are not reflected in the personal income levels of the metropolitan area. Similarly, a great deal of profit may accrue to the event organizers or the participants in the game, neither of whom are likely to be local citizens. Indeed, while the regional or national effects of the Super Bowl may be large, the local economic impact appears to be quite small, but it is the local residents that are normally expected to bear the brunt of costs associated with hosting the event.

Table 6. Probabilities for Various Levels of Economic Impact Induced by the Super Bowl

Economic impact	Probability of such an impact or greater having occurred
$400 million	0.87%
$392.8 million	1.00%
$300 million	5.00%
$252.7 million	10.00%
$200 million	19.28%
$100 million	47.40%
$91.9 million	50.00%
$0	77.00%
Negative	23.00%

Conclusions and Policy Implications

The National Football League and other sports leagues have used the promise of an all star game or league championship as an incentive for host cities to construct new stadiums or arenas and, with few exceptions, at considerable public expense. Recent NFL studies have estimated that Super Bowls increase economic activity by hundreds of millions of dollars in host cities. Our analysis fails to support NFL claims. Our detailed regression analysis revealed that over the period 1970 to 2001, on average Super Bowls created $92 million in income gains for host cities, a figure roughly one-quarter that of recent NFL claims. While this figure, like any econometric estimate, is subject to some degree of uncertainty, statistical analysis reveals that, on average the Super Bowl could not have contributed, by a reasonable standard of statistical significance, more than $300 million to host economies.

Cities would be wise to view with caution Super Bowl economic impact estimates provided by the NFL. It would appear that padding is an essential element of the game both on and off the field.

Acknowledgements

This paper is a revision of a paper presented at the Western Economic Association International 79th annual conference, Vancouver, 2 July 2004, in a session organized by Brad Humphreys, University of Illinois. The authors are grateful for the comments and suggestions made by session participants as well as two anonymous referees.

Notes

1. Steeg claimed that the NFL and NFL Properties spend a combined $43 million on Super Bowl XXXIV, for example.
2. At the March 1999 NFL meetings, the teams agreed to allow teams to qualify for up-front loans in an amount equal to 34% to 50% of the private contributions for stadium projects. The specific amount would be determined by the size of the project and the market the stadium would serve (NFL, 1999a).
3. Porter's use of monthly sales receipts is important. If the researcher can compress the time period, then it is less likely that the impact of the event will be obscured by the large, diverse economy within which it took place. The use of annual data has the potential to mask an event's impact through the sheer weight of activity that occurs in large economies over the course of a year unless steps are taken to isolate the event.
4. Note that the term "multiplier" here refers to static input-output multipliers rather than the Keynesian macroeconomic multiplier based upon an economy's marginal propensity to consume.

References

Arthur Anderson (2000). Hospitality and leisure services. The Sydney Olympic performance Survey: The Sydney Olympic Games on the Australian Hotel Industry. *Mimeograph*, 1–7.

Baade, R. (1996). Professional sports as a catalyst for metropolitan economic development. *Journal of Urban Affairs, 18*(1), 1–17.

Baade, R., & Matheson, V. (2000). An assessment of the economic impact of the American Football Championship, the Super Bowl, on host communities. *Reflets et Perspectives, 39*(2–3), 35–46.

Coates, D., & Humphreys, B. (2002). The economic impact of post-season play in professional sports. *Journal of Sports Economics, 3*(3), 291–299.

Coates, D. (2006). The tax benefits of hosting the Super Bowl and the MLB All-Star Game: the Houston experience, *International Journal of Sport Finance, 1*(4).

Davidson, L. (1999). Choice of a proper methodology to measure quantitative and qualitative effects of the impact of sport. In C. Jeanrenaud (Ed.), *The Economic Impact of Sports Events* (pp. 9–28). Neuchatel, Switzerland: Centre International d'Etude du Sport.

Humphreys, J. (1994). The economic impact of hosting Super Bowl XXVIII on Georgia. *Georgia Business and Economic Conditions*, May–June, 18–21.

Matheson, V. (2004). Economic multipliers and mega-event analysis. College of the Holy Cross, Department of Economics Working Paper No. 04–02, June.

Mills, E., & McDonald, J. (Eds.) (1992). *Sources of Metropolitan Growth*. New Brunswick, NJ: Center for Urban Policy Research.

National Football League (1999a). Eagles, steelers make plans for new stadiums. *NFL Report, 58*(3).

National Football League (1999b). Super Bowl XXXII generates $396 million for South Florida. *NFL Report, 58*(7).

Peter, J. (2002). Building NFL fortunes. *The Times-Picayune*, Section C, p. 1, 14 July.

Porter, P. (1999). Mega-sports events as municipal investments: A critique of impact analysis. In J. Fizel, E. Gustafson, & L. Hadley (Eds.) (1999). *Sports Economics: Current Research*. New York: Praeger Press.

Siegfried, J., & Zimbalist, A. (2002). A note on the local economic impact of sports expenditures. *Journal of Sports Economics, 3*(4), 361–366.

Steeg, J. (1999). Inquiring minds should know. *Fox Sports Biz.com*, 9 November.

Growth Impact of Major Sporting Events

ELMER STERKEN

University of Groningen, the Netherlands

In this paper we analyse the economic impact of organizing the Summer Olympic Games and the FIFA Football World Cup (World Cup in brief hereafter). These two events are the largest sporting events in the world (measured by attendance and financing needs) and have a strong international following in terms of (pre-)competition and participation. Although the Olympic Summer Games is characterized by a large variety of sports, while the World Cup involves only football, both events attract huge media attention rates and require substantial budgets. One major issue for hosting cities (and so national authorities) is whether significant additional economic growth effects can be derived from efficient organization. In the literature so far no systematic evidence of multiple events across different countries has been presented, but in this paper a first attempt is made.

Economic analyses show mixed evidence as to whether organizing large sporting events contributes to economic growth. There is a lively debate on the size and direction of impact on the development of local economic activity (i.e. within cities or counties). Local organizers tend to produce optimistic *ex-ante* forecasts, using cost–benefit analyses based on, for example, input-output or computable general equilibrium models, and predict a serious growth impact. *Ex-post* analyses, measuring observed changes in factors such as (local) income and attributing these changes to the impact of hosting a sporting event are, on average, more modest. There are various explanations of the different findings between *ex-ante* and *ex-post* studies (see, e.g., Baade & Matheson, 2004a). First is the crowding out argument: in *ex-ante* analyses often the gross result is confused with net impact. Second, the precise impact of the so-called income multiplier might be wrongly estimated. Moreover, analyses based on surveys of inhabitants of cities or regions can be affected by selection bias: opinions of those who do not respond are as important to the final result as the opinions of those who do respond.

In this paper we contribute to the debate on the impact of major sporting events by presenting *ex-post* evidence. Our main contribution is that we pursue the analysis on major sporting events on a national instead of a regional level. We consider the two largest sporting events, the Summer Olympic Games and the World Cup and analyse their impact on national economic development. Thus we do not focus on national sporting events, such as the Super Bowl or the Oxford–Cambridge Boat Race, or on other large international events, such as the UEFA Champions League Final, the IAAF World Championships in Athletics, the Winter Olympic Games or the UEFA European Cup Football (see, e.g., Oldenboom (2006) for an analysis of the Euro Cup 2000 in Belgium and the Netherlands). The latter international events have recently attracted substantial attention, but are still far smaller than the Summer Olympic Games and World Cup in terms of media exposure, costs and revenues. Moreover, the Winter Olympic Games and UEFA Cup attract a smaller number of countries in participation (both in the event and in pre-competition) than the Summer Olympic Games and World Cup. Local single- or multiple-day events also are smaller in financial size than the two major sporting events we consider.

The interest in the macroeconomic impact of organizing events such as the Olympic Summer Games and the World Cup has increased as bidding cities want to present a balanced view of their expected costs and benefits. Organizing major sporting events such as these requires approximately 10 to 20 billion US dollars (of which the operating costs are only a fraction and investment costs have increased substantially over the years). Both public (national and local governments and, e.g., the IOC or FIFA) and private sources of finance (sponsors) are used as financiers. The share of broadcasting and sponsorship revenues in financing the events has increased over the years (see Preuss, 2004, for evidence on the Olympic Summer Games), while ticketing revenues have decreased in relative importance. Given the enormous financial burden of organizing major sporting events, a positive macroeconomic impact is of course advantageous (if positive) to local bidding organizations.

The impact of organizing major sporting events on local economic activity is a topic of significant debate. Arguments relating to both supply (via investment in infrastructure, telecommunications, labour productivity, and urban development) and demand (increase in tourism, consumer confidence, local availability of jobs) contribute to explaining changes in (local) growth rates. However, demand effects might lead to crowding out, even at the regional level and certainly at the national level. Establishing supply effects is most likely to be affected by the omitted variable problem. Even on the regional/city level there is a serious debate about the evidence of the economic impact of organizing sporting events. In the following section we present a short review of this literature and focus on the distinction between *ex-ante* and *ex-post* analyses. Next we present an overall combined cross-section time-series approach to analyse the macroeconomic impact of major events. We use data over both the full history of the Modern Olympic Summer Games and the World Cup in a descriptive setting and in a model of the post-war sample, in most cases from 1960 onwards, to establish the impact of major sporting events on (per capita) GDP (gross domestic product)-growth rates. We present the descriptive analysis in the third section and an economic panel growth model in the fourth section. The fifth section presents a summary and conclusions.

Modelling the Impact of Major Sporting Events

There are two types of economic analyses to establish the impact of organizing major sporting events on (local) economic development. First, one can predict the expected impact using an *ex-ante* analysis. Most organizing committees produce such forecasts. As with any other economic forecasting experiment, various types of error can cause forecasts to differ from outcomes. First, there might be model uncertainty. In the analysis of the economic impact of large sporting events, input–output or computable general equilibrium models are popular tools to integrate economic impact analysis into a cost–benefit setting, but all types of models have their analytical strengths and weaknesses. Besides the functional form of the model, model parameters might also be subject to uncertainty. If model parameters are, for instance, not invariant to large shocks, such as the organization of a major sporting event, predictions based on historical parameters may lead to erroneous conclusions. Next there is uncertainty in model variables. Forecasting requires the input of expected time paths of the exogenous variables, which might not materialize in practice. Moreover, some relevant variables might not be included in the model. Third, related to variability of model parameters, economic agents might change their behaviour due to the shock of occurrence of the event. This implies that the proposed model is not capable of estimating the behavioural consequences due to dependence on policy.

The second type of analysis is *ex post*, establishing the contribution of the organization of large sporting events to economic development. This type of *ex-post* analysis is not subject to uncertainty in the development of exogenous model variables, or unforeseen changes in behaviour, but is still dependent on the choice of the (conditioning) model. Take, for example, a simple econometric model that models economic growth as a function of 'normal' economic growth determinants and an indicator of the sporting event. First, there might be an omitted variable problem in the set of growth determinants. Next, endogeneity of both the growth determinants and the organization of the event might blur the results. An example would be that a local organization committee of the World Cup which selects a city to host matches that is expected to have a prosperous future. If local growth materializes it may be due to the projected prosperity of the city rather than the hosting of games. So, even if models seek to control for the above mentioned crowding out and biased estimation of the multipliers (if relevant), there may still be differences between *ex-ante* and *ex-post* studies. Finally, there may be political factors at play: local organizers sometimes only publish or use optimistic analyses.

There is a large literature on both *ex-ante* and *ex-post* studies of the economic impact of sporting events. Many studies of the Summer Olympic Games are present in the *ex-ante* class (see Preuss, 2004, p. 45 for a review). As Preuss illustrates for the Summer Olympic Games, there is empirical evidence on the estimated economic impact since the Munich 1972 Games (see, e.g., studies such as Humphreys & Plummer (1995) for the Atlanta 1996 Games, Andersen (1999) for the Sydney 2000 Olympics, and Papanikos (1999) for the Athens 2004 Games). *Ex-ante* studies for the World Cup have been carried out as well such as by; Goodman & Stern (1994) for the US edition of the World Cup in 1994 and Ahlert (2001) and Rahmann & Kurscheidt (2002) for the World Cup in Germany in 2006.

Next there are *ex-post* studies of the organization of sporting events. Examples for the World Cup are Baade & Matheson (2004a) for the US 1994 World Cup and Kim *et al.* (2006) for the World Cup 2002 in Korea. For the Olympic Games, Baade &Matheson (2002) propose a methodology to assess the economic impact on the city level and Hotchkiss *et al.* (2003) give an analysis of local employment and wage changes during the 1996 Atlanta Summer Games. There are several other *ex- post* studies of the impact of organizing local sporting events, such as the Super Bowl (see Porter, 1999; Baade & Matheson, 2000, 2004b; Matheson, 2005), the Major League Baseball All-Star Game (Baade & Matheson, 2001), post-season American professional sports (Siegfried & Zimbalist, 2000; Coates & Humphreys, 2002) on the economic development of the host city. The studies on the Super Bowl event are examples of the debate on the magnitude of the local economic impact of the organization of this event in the US and demonstrate a large range of possible outcomes. The *ex-post* studies on average are modest with respect to the conclusion whether the organization of the sporting events contributes to per capita income of the inhabitants of the host city.

In this study we combine sporting event data in a time frame and so lump together different national institutions. Such a multi-country approach has pros and cons. The most important disadvantage is probably that we consider heterogeneous events. Each event tells a different story and averaging out probably destroys valuable information. On the other hand, a cross-section study delivers systematic "evidence" at the macroeconomic level. Since event-specific circumstances are so crucial to the outcome of the analysis, individual results are probably less relevant to future decisions, while a cross-event study does contribute to supplying such information. *Ex-post*-cross-event analysis of course crucially depends on appropriate conditioning of economic results for "normal" economic development.

Organizing a major sporting event like the Olympic Summer Games or the World Cup is believed to have a national economic impact. Below we briefly review the likely transmission channels of a sports shock (see, e.g., Price Waterhouse Coopers, 2004, or Preuss 2004, for detailed discussions). We shortly review the channels of transmission from organizing a large sporting event on economic conditions. We classify the channels according to the following characteristics:

1. What are the *ex-ante*, during, and *ex-post* channels of influence?
2. Which mechanisms affect technology (e.g. the capital stock, use of labour and technological progress) or preferences (by home and foreign agents (tourism) in terms of supply of labour and consumption behaviour) or both?
3. What are the complex social interactions which result from success, over-optimism and other behavioural channels?

Empirical evidence discussed above suggests that the overall economic impact of large-scale events is difficult to evaluate due to the multiple channels at work. Note that, on the world level, there will be no impact of organizing local sporting events. So we consider local shifts of economic activity at best. Since we do not link the "shocks" of organizing major sporting events to deep structural technology or preference descriptions, and we do not stress behavioural elements in great detail, we focus on the timing of the impact. Concerning the timing, we can observe the following alleged benefits:

• It is likely that *ex-ante* investment will increase. In most cases new sporting facilities and infrastructure need to be constructed. This holds to a larger extent for the Summer Olympic Games than for the World Cup, because the Summer Olympics include many different sporting events and require more non-sporting infrastructure. It seems to matter whether investment is private or public, what the expected returns in general will be (probably dependent on the type of investment), and how investment can be financed (by issuing bonds, using retained private earnings, equity issues, etc.). Siegfried & Zimbalist (2000) doubt the economic impact of investment in infrastructural facilities such as stadiums. Well-known debates in this class are of the following nature: in bidding for the Olympic Games one can question the need for new buildings and roads (especially their return after the end of the Games) knowing that both the private and public sector were unwilling to invest without organizing the Games; sometimes, the organization of a large event is simply a short-run reduction of the uncertainty premium on waiting to invest; in addition tourism will increase: people are curious to see the new stadium, etc.

- Consumer expenditure will increase during the event. Tourism will boost expenditure. Depending on local wage flexibility, mark-ups will increase, employment will boom and local profits will increase. Probably consumer confidence will be boosted, especially if the national team(s) or sportsmen perform well (see Ashton *et al.*, 2003) for an example of the relation between sports success and the stock exchange). Local receipts (e.g. ticketing) and other sources of revenues will have at least a short-run multiplier impact on the local economy.
- After the major event has come to an end, the local economy can benefit from the (temporary) demand shock and the increased quality of infrastructure. Probably reputation also plays a role: the name of the city can, for example, turn into a brand name. Human capital can probably be increased in quality, and urban regeneration might increase the tourist value of the organizing cities.

On the cost side we should keep in mind the opportunity costs: the same money could have been spent on other things. *Ex-ante*, investment costs and so-called preparatory costs (say the costs of bidding) will be important. During the event there are operational costs, such as the costs to keep the event safe, and after the event maintenance costs might come to the fore. In all three instances the various arguments might apply differently to the various cities or nations.

From a macroeconomic theory perspective one could expect the investment in infrastructure and human capital to have permanent effects on economic growth. For some cases this evidence seems to hold. Famous examples are the economic development of Seoul after 1988 and Barcelona after 1992. These cities seem to have benefited from better infrastructure and telecommunications, as well as city renovation, to a large extent. However, these effects seem to be local and cannot be observed at the national level. Temporary increases in demand via tourism seem to be influential in explaining demand shocks, which typically have shorter horizon propagation functions. Tourism may be boosted during the event. At the 2002 World Cup more than 1 million tourists visited Korea. On the other hand congestion forecasts might force non-sports tourists to postpone their visit (this is known to have been the case for Athens 2004). The revenues from operations have a modest impact, since a large fraction of the receipts goes to international and foreign organizations.

The impact of over-optimism on factors such as consumer spending is another channel of a demand effect. This effect is really temporary. Investigating indexes of OECD consumer confidence for Italy 1990, Barcelona 1992, France 1998 and Athens 2004 reveals that only in the French case was consumer confidence boosted. As Falter *et al.* (2005) show, this had an impact on the demand for football (in terms of demand for tickets for the national league after 1998). However, for the other cases there is no clear behavioral change in consumer behaviour.

Descriptive Economic Growth Statistics

In order to get a first impression of the macroeconomic impact of organizing major sporting events such as the Summer Olympic Games and World Cup we compute over time the GDP growth rates of the organizing countries. For this element we used an historical GDP data set developed by Maddison (2003). For major economies we have GDP-data from 1870 onwards (including data for the Soviet Union). From this set we computed a weighted average world growth rate and denoted this average rate as world GDP growth. Next we corrected national growth rates for the world GDP growth rate (by deduction) and use a 15-year window of the median excess growth rates of the organizing countries to analyse the relation between the major sporting event and economic growth. So our cases consisted of 15 observations ($t-7,\ldots,t,\ldots,t+7$) of excess growth rates of real GDP of the organizing country per event. We make a distinction between the Olympic Games and the World Cup in Table 1. For the Olympic Games we started the sample in 1900 (the Paris edition); for the World Cup we started with the Italian edition of 1934. We stopped at the Athens 2004 edition for the Olympic Games and the 2002 Korea/Japan edition of the World Cup (otherwise we would have had too few observations on future data). We split data for the Olympic Games into three categories, editions before 1956, the editions between 1956 and 1984, and the more recent ones (after 1984). For the World Cup we divided the sample into three editions before 1954, between 1954 and 1978 and the editions after 1978. Note that for the results with respect to the Olympic Games the editions in Japan 1964 and Korea 1988 increase the mean and median growth rates in the sub-sample after 1956. The general pattern remains the same however: the countries hosting the Olympic Games seem to have higher GDP growth rates than the World Cup hosts.

The table shows two principal findings. Note that the figures are in percentage-point deviations from the median growth rate (we take the median instead of the mean to account for skewness of the distributions). The first finding is that if there is any impact of any event on macroeconomic growth in this simple setting, it is insignificant. The second finding is that standard deviations of the median excess growth rates are about 1.5 to 2% GDP-growth. This finding illustrates that we need to explain economic growth better in order to understand the impact of major sporting events. This is the goal of the analysis in the next section, where we estimate a growth model including organizing major sporting events dummy variables. The variance of the excess GDP-growth of the old editions of the Olympic Games and the World Cup is by far larger, but the overall impact is modest due to the size and technology of the events in those years. Second, the impact of the Olympic Games exceeds the impact of the World Cup. Over the 15-year window the excess median GDP growth rate of those countries that organized the Olympic Games is about one percentage point higher than the corresponding values for the countries staging the World Cup. For the Olympic Games we clearly see the investment effect prior to the event, and

Table 1. Median Excess Real GDP Growth Rates

Period	Olympic Games	Before 1956	1956–1984	After 1984	World Cup	Before 1954	1954–1978	After 1978
$t-7$	0.631	−0.935	1.284	−0.682	−0.747	−2.758	0.184	−0.538
$t-6$	−0.350	−0.528	0.341	−0.492	−1.208	1.061	−1.666	−1.208
$t-5$	−0.667	−3.176	−0.614	−0.256	−0.137	4.729	−0.137	−0.966
$t-4$	0.214	1.030	0.054	0.144	−1.978	−1.978	−0.479	−2.002
$t-3$	0.942	0.401	0.942	1.241	−2.007	−0.484	−1.166	−2.352
$t-2$	0.521	−0.035	0.955	1.345	−0.934	1.396	−0.958	−0.934
$t-1$	0.600	0.016	0.809	0.644	−0.412	1.111	0.003	−1.125
t	−0.759	−1.593	1.101	−1.077	−0.728	−0.831	−2.109	−0.159
$t+1$	−0.627	−1.970	−0.606	−0.323	−0.813	0.613	0.000	−1.535
$t+2$	1.405	2.722	1.038	1.010	−1.048	−7.256	0.609	−1.298
$t+3$	−0.504	−1.139	0.108	−0.314	−0.659	−0.041	−1.368	−0.659
$t+4$	−1.208	−1.763	−0.499	−1.563	−0.497	0.271	−1.328	−0.492
$t+5$	−0.896	−0.924	−1.025	−0.867	0.727	0.727	0.415	0.744
$t+6$	−0.648	−1.194	−0.152	1.374	−1.548	−3.318	−0.964	−1.548
$t+7$	0.147	−0.418	0.254	0.544	−1.818	4.636	−1.714	−2.336

Note: The figures are in percentage-points deviations from the world real GDP growth average. Source of the data: Maddison (2003). The first editions included are the 1900 Paris edition of the Olympic Games and the 1934 Italy edition of the World Cup. The last edition of the Olympic Games included is Athens 2004, while for the World Cup Japan/Korea 2002 is the last event.

to a lesser extent the legacy effect after the games. However, the basic findings of Table 1 are purely descriptive and should be complemented by a growth analysis. The growth analysis can increase the probability of finding statistically significant results by conditioning economic growth for its standard determinants.

A Simple Growth Model Including the Timing of Major Sporting Events

In the previous section we explored economic growth of the countries organizing the two major sporting events, the Summer Olympic Games and the World Cup. There is weak (insignificant) evidence that the organizers of the Summer Olympic Games have rather prosperous rates of economic growth, while this is not true for the World Cup. There can be two objections to these descriptive observations. First, one should correct growth rates for the "normal" growth rates of the economies involved. Second, it could be that the International Olympic Committee (IOC) has simply selected higher growth-potential countries to organize the Summer Olympic Games than the FIFA did for the World Cup. Indeed this might be a problem for the Summer Olympic Games. The IOC uses the ability of future organizers to build the appropriate accommodation as one of its decision-making criteria. This implies that expected economic growth indeed might be relevant to the choice of the host country. Up until 1994 FIFA selected in turn a European country and a Latin-American country to host the tournament four years later. This reduces the selection bias for the World Cup to some extent. After 1994 FIFA adopted has a global policy of selecting a country from each continent in succession, so that development of football as a sport dominates the decision. In order to test this selection bias hypothesis we estimated a binary choice (logit) model with the event dummy variables as dependent variables (taking the value 1 if a country organized an event and 0 in other cases) and lagged GDP per capita growth as determinants. There is no endogeneity of the events found for lags up to eight years.

In order to solve the first problem we needed to condition the correlations for other determinants of economic growth. We included the organization of major sporting events in a simple empirical growth model. Since the work of Barro & Lee (1994) and Barro & Sala-I-Martin (1998), economic growth models have been tested extensively. The main debate in this class of models concentrates on the selection of growth determinants and the modelling of convergence. We do not want to contribute to this discussion and merely use the framework of economic growth models to explore conditioned correlations between economic growth and major sporting events dummy variables. Economic growth models have the form:

$$\Delta y_{it} = \alpha \, y_{it,.base} + \beta \, X_{it} + \gamma_i + \delta_t + \varepsilon_{it} \qquad (1)$$

where y_{it} represents the log of GDP per capita in country i in year t, $y_{it.base}$ is the log of GDP per capita in a fixed base year (but which is included for each estimation period to control for the impact of differences in growth rates at the beginning of the sample), X_{it} a set of determinants (including for instance dummy variables indicating the organization of a sporting event), γ_i country specific effects, δ_t time specific effects and ε_{it} residuals. The time specific effects can be interpreted as average world economic growth (and other possible universal trends). The inclusion of these fixed coefficients therefore makes the results of the growth model comparable to the descriptive exercise in the previous section, where we corrected growth rates for the world average. The theory of convergence concentrates on α, which relates per capita growth rate of GDP with the level of GDP per capita in the base year. Countries with a relatively low GDP per capita have more growth potential. The discussion on the empirical growth models centres on the selection of the determinants, the specification of the time intervals (such as the use of annual data, five-year averages, or even longer time spans), and the way to estimate the models. Concerning the selection of growth determinants, the most likely candidates are indicators of investment in physical and human capital. The latter variables are typically hard to measure at a high frequency, as in our case, which renders them useless in an annual event-window analysis. Besides investment indicators, indicators of openness of the economy are often found to be relevant. There is also evidence that monetary conditions affect economic growth. In our model we include, therefore, gross fixed capital formation, trade as a percentage of GDP, and the inflation rate as growth determinants. Note that we are not so much interested in the individual contribution of these normal growth determinants (and so collinearity between the standard growth determinants is uninteresting as long as they do not correlate with the event dummy variables), but merely concentrate on the variables that indicate the organization of a major sporting event.

We estimate a pooled time series cross-section model (1) and include dummy variables for the large events for a four-year window (we use 4 instead of 7 lags and leads due to the number of observations available). We test for the suitability of a fixed versus random effects specification of the model and find that fixed effects cannot be rejected. We used data from the World Development Indicators from the World Bank. This set is available for 208 countries from 1960 onwards, and allows us to get consistent data on GDP per capita, gross fixed capital formation, and trade data (the Maddison (2003) data set only includes GDP data, but for a longer time span). We have reduced the set of 208 countries to 96 countries that have actively participated in both the Summer Olympic Games and the World Cup. This means that we have included countries that have never organized one of the two major sporting events, but could be potential candidates for hosting (the main assumption being that participation signals the desire to organize). This extends the descriptive statistics in the previous section, where we only included observations on countries which had organized one of the two events. Our dependent variable is the first difference of the log of real GDP per capita. Note that this is slightly different to the real GDP-growth rate data used in the third section. However, the main variation originates from fluctuations in real GDP and not in population. In growth models it is common to use the growth rate of real GDP per capita as dependent variable. We included the 1960 level of real GDP per capita (in 1995 US dollars) $\log(GDP_{60})$, the growth rate of the gross real fixed capital formation as a percentage of real GDP $\Delta\log(GFC)$, the log of the trade share of GDP $\log(TRA)$, and the inflation rate INF as base determinants. Next we included dummy variables, denoted by $t+i$, where i runs from –4 to 4, to denote the organization of major sporting events and use a four-year window. Table 2 presents the major findings. We show that adding the event dummy variables improves the fit of the model (as one can see from the reduction of the sum of squared residuals SSR). The signs of the determinants are as expected: gross fixed capital formation contributes to economic growth, as does trade openness, while inflation has a negative impact. The insignificant parameter estimates of $\log(GDP_{60})$ denotes that we do not find evidence of convergence.

Table 2 includes results for a base model without event dummy variables, a column for the Summer Olympic Games and one for the World Cup. It shows some remarkable results. First, the values of the dummy variable parameters are relatively large in some cases, up to 2.5 percentage-points in the current year. This suggests that the per capita growth rates around the date of organizing major sporting events have varied substantially from a normal growth rate. Given some of the cautions of estimating growth models to be discussed hereafter, the absolute figures should be interpreted with care. The high growth differentials could be due to selection bias. Take, for instance, the case of Japan 1964 or Korea 1988: both economies were booming in the years around their event dates, which effect is not fully controlled for by including the 1960 per capita GDP level (Japanese and Korean values were rather low then) or the other three determinants. Second, the difference between the Summer Olympic Games and the World Cup is remarkable. We find very positive additional real growth rates for the impact of organizing the Summer Olympic Games, but no or negative effects for the World Cup.

A few words of caution should be made in interpreting the estimation results. First, the growth model might not be conditioned properly: relevant variables explaining economic growth of the 96 economies might still be omitted. In addition, some of the growth determinants might be endogenous, which would require other econometric techniques (e.g. using instrumental variables). There might also be a selection bias in our set of 96 countries, as we exclude countries that did not participate in both events in the past. A final point of critique on the growth model could be that the event dummy variables are endogenous. As noted before the cities or countries selected are known about seven years in advance in our sample, though our test results indicate exogeneity.

As in Table 1, with descriptive statistics we performed estimation in the corresponding sub-samples (1964–1980 and 1984–1998 for the Olympic Games, and 1964–1978 and 1982–1998 for the World Cup) as a robustness check of our main findings in Table 2. The results are in Table 3. Table 3 shows that the general conclusions of Table 2 still hold. If anything, the

Table 2. Pooled Estimation Results: Real GDP Per Capita Growth

Variable	Base model	Olympic Games	World Cup
$\log(GDP_{60})$	−0.186	−0.181	−0.192
	(−1.168)	(−1.126)	(−1.200)
$\Delta (\log(GFC))$	6.052*	6.043*	6.039*
	(6.315)	(6.297)	(6.352)
$\log(TRA)$	2.528*	2.513*	2.482*
	(3.842)	(3.793)	(3.696)
INF	−7.182*	−7.167*	−7.179*
	(−3.532)	(−3.530)	(−3.533)
$t-4$		1.730	0.368
		(1.489)	(0.450)
$t-3$		1.924*	−1.437*
		(2.178)	(−2.443)
$t-2$		1.515*	−1.511*
		(2.364)	(−2.098)
$t-1$		−0.426	0.184
		(0.610)	(0.167)
t		2.499*	−2.385
		(2.848)	(−1.846)
$t+1$		1.936*	−0.978
		(2.295)	(−1.355)
$t+2$		1.442	−1.002
		(1.586)	(−1.031)
$t+3$		1.025*	−2.168*
		(2.813)	(−2.568)
$t+4$		1.163	−2.409
		(1.219)	(−1.574)
R^2	0.230	0.229	0.230
SSR	43882	43784	43741
Countries		96	
Years		1964–1998	
Country-year observations		2618	

Notes: Effective sample: 1964–1998. The dependent variable is in percentages. We denote significance of the parameters at the 5% confidence level by a *; *t*-values based on White-consistent estimation are within parentheses. R^2 is the adjusted coefficient of determination. *SSR* denotes the sum of squared residuals and indicates the goodness of fit of the model. Country and time specific fixed effects are not shown.

Olympic Games turn out to have a positive impact on economic growth, while this does not hold for the World Cup. The significance of the event dummy variables drops, though, mainly because the number of observations decreases in the sub-samples. Again, this illustrates that we should interpret the findings in Table 2 with caution. Table 3 shows that for the 1964–1980 sample the current-year (*t*) impact is significantly positive, while for the 1984–1998 sub-sample the (*t*+2)-impact is positive. For the World Cup we

Table 3. Pooled Estimation Results: Real GDP Per Capita Growth (Sub-samples)

	Olympic Games		World Cup	
Variable	1964–1980	1984–1998	1964–1978	1982–1998
$\log(GDP_{60})$	0.306	−0.127	0.243	−0.248
	(0.886)	(−0.361)	(0.570)	(−0.812)
$\Delta\,(\log(GFC))$	4.634*	5.902*	3.200*	6.269*
	(2.746)	(4.904)	(2.082)	(5.299)
$\log(TRA)$	3.041*	1.784*	3.133*	2.341*
	(2.348)	(1.314)	(2.071)	(2.100)
INF	−0.238*	−7.013*	−0.238*	−7.213*
	(−4.397)	(−3.430)	(−3.740)	(3.487)
$t-4$	3.308	0.300	0.845	0.387
	(1.452)	(0.353)	(0.450)	(0.561)
$t-3$	1.528	1.740	−1.841	−0.769
	(0.658)	(1.536)	(−1.680)	(−1.048)
$t-2$	1.378	1.417	−0.522	−1.740*
	(0.581)	(1.679)	(−0.445)	(3.240)
$t-1$	−1.937	0.104	−1.175	−0.566
	(−1.021)	(0.107)	(−1.152)	(−1.668)
t	3.321*	1.881	−2.512	−1.415
	(3.708)	(1.551)	(−1.365)	(−1.136)
$t+1$	−0.464	1.744	0.362	−0.565
	(−0.865)	(1.379)	(0.140)	(−1.011)
$t+2$	0.047	2.534*	1.586	−0.378
	(0.056)	(3.056)	(1.419)	(−0.551)
$t+3$	0.549	0.883	−0.073	−1.768
	(0.668)	(0.655)	(−0.061)	(−1.582)
$t+4$	0.881	0.964	−0.782	−3.140
	(0.307)	(1.325)	(−0.779)	(−1.534)
R^2	0.154	0.265	0.128	0.278
SSR	18838	18235	15585	20880
Countries	78	96	76	96
Years	1964–1980	1984–1998	1964–1978	1982–1998
Observations	997	1367	844	1536

Notes: Effective sample: 1964–1998. The dependent variable is in percentages. We denote significance of the parameters at the 5% confidence level by a *; t-values based on White-consistent estimation are within parentheses. R^2 is the adjusted coefficient of determination. SSR denotes the sum of squared residuals and indicates the goodness of fit of the model. Country and time specific fixed effects are not shown.

only find a $(t-2)$ negative impact for the 1982–1998 editions. One can see that the growth model produces a better fit in the more recent years.

Both Tables 2 and 3 show that there is a positive contribution in organizing the Summer Olympic Games and a slightly negative impact in organizing the World Cup. It is interesting to note what may explain the differences between the Olympic Games and the World Cup. First of all it might be that the International Olympic Committee selects higher growth potential economies to organize the Summer Olympic Games than FIFA does for the World Cup, as discussed above. It is clear that the IOC has had more degrees of freedom in selecting the host country than FIFA. Next, it is accepted that the Olympic Games need more investment (due to the large variety of sports), which demands a more careful selection of the hosting city or country. The investment itself also generates growth effects in the years prior to the event, and most likely also afterwards due to improvements in infrastructure. In football, in some cases, the stadiums are available and need only to be renovated. Moreover, access to the stadiums is mostly available, which reduces the investment in infrastructure.

Summary and Conclusions

Organizing major sporting events can boost local economic activity. According to a popular view, investment in infrastructure, a boost in current consumption and an increase in consumer confidence lead to extra growth opportunities. Empirical studies so far do not come to a unified conclusion with respect to the economic impact of major sporting events. Using a post-war growth model we show that a positive impact might hold for the Olympic Games, but not for the FIFA World Cup. Our panel approach is the first in analysing *ex post* the macroeconomic contribution of organizing major sporting events and presents an alternative to event-specific *ex-ante* analyses. We have used simple descriptive statistics for a long time span and a pooled fixed effects model to compare the economic impact of the Summer Games and the World Cup on per capita GDP-growth rates. The growth model suggests that economic growth rates have been higher in those countries that hosted the Olympic Summer Games than in countries that organized the World Cup. These findings suggest caution in claims relating particularly to the economic benefits of staging the World Cup; however we should acknowledge that our approach is too general for individual bidding processes, because individual circumstances will probably be of larger influence to local economic development.

References

Ahlert, G. (2001). The economic effects of the Soccer World Cup 2006 in Germany with regard to different financing. *Economic Systems Research*, 13(1), 110–118.

Andersen, A. (1999). Economic impact study of the Sydney 2000 Olympic Games. Centre for Regional Economic Analysis Tasmania, Working Paper.

Ashton, J. K., Gerrard, B., & Hudson, R. (2003). Economic impact of national sporting success: The London Stock Exchange. *Applied Economics Letters*, 10, 783–785.

Baade, R. A., & Matheson, V. A. (2000). An assessment of the economic impact of the American Football Championship, the Super Bowl, on host communities. *Reflets et Perspectives de La Vie Économique*, 39(2–3), 35–46.

Baade, R. A., & Matheson, V. A. (2001). Home run or wild pitch? Assessing the economic impact of Major League Baseball's All-Star Game. *Journal of Sports Economics*, 2(4), 307–327.

Baade, R. A., & Matheson, V. A. (2002). Bidding for the Olympics: Fool's Gold? In C. P. Barros, M. Ibrahímo, & S. Szymanski (Eds.), *Transatlantic Sport: The Comparative Economics of North American and European Sports*(pp. 127–151). Cheltenham, UK, and Northampton/MA: Edward Elgar.

Baade, R. A., & Matheson, V. A. (2004a). The quest for the cup: assessing the economic impact of the World Cup. *Regional Studies, 38*(4), 343–354.

Baade, R. A., & Matheson, V. A. (2004b). Super Bowl or Super (Hyper)Bole: the economic impact of the Super Bowl on host communities. *College of the Holy Cross Working Paper* 04–03.

Barro, R., & Lee, J. W. (1994). Sources of economic growth. *Carnegie-Rochester Conference Series on Public Policy, 40,* 1–46.

Barro, R., & Sala-I-Martin, X. (1998). *Economic Growth.* Cambridge, MA: MIT Press.

Coates, D., & Humphreys, B. R. (2002). The economic impact of post-season play in professional sports. *Journal of Sports Economics, 3*(3), 291–299.

Falter, J.-M., Pérignon, C., & Vercruysse, O. (2005). Impact of overwhelming joy on consumer demand: the case of a Soccer World-Cup victory. University of Geneva: Discussion Paper.

Goodman, R. & Stern, R. (1994). Chicago hosts opening game of the World Cup. *Illinois Parks and Recreation, 25,* 3.

Hotchkiss, J. L., Moore, R.E., & Zobey, S. M. (2003). Impact of 1996 Summer Olympic Games on Employment and wages in Georgia. *Southern Economic Journal, 69*(3), 691–704.

Humphreys, J. M., & Plummer, M. K. (1995). The economic impact on the state of Georgia of hosting the 1996 Olympic Games. Selig Center for Economic Growth. Georgia, Studies and Forecasts.

Kim, H. Y., Gursoy, D., & Lee, S.-B. (2006). The impact of the 2002 World Cup on South Korea: comparisons of pre- and post-Games. *Tourism Management, 27,* 86–96.

Kim. Y., Rhee, S.-W., Yu, J.-C., Koo, K.-M., & Hong, J.-D. (1989). Impact of the Seoul Olympic Games on Korean economic development, Korea Development Institute, Working Paper 1989–05.

Maddison, A. (2003). *The World Economy: Historical Statistics.* Paris: OECD.

Matheson, V. A. (2005). Contrary evidence on the economic effect of the Super Bowl on the victorious city. *Journal of Sports Economics, 6*(4), 420–428.

Oldenboom, E (2006). *Cost and Benefits of Major Sports Events.* Amsterdam: MeerWaarde Onderzoeksadvies.

Papanikos, T. (1999). The economic impact of international iourism and the Olympic Games of Athens 2004. Athens Institute of Education and Research, Study Series.

Porter, P. (1999). Mega-sports events as municipal investments: a critique of impact analysis. In J. L. Fizel, E. Gustafson, & L. Hadley (Eds.), *Sports Economics: Current Research.* Westport, CT: Praeger Press.

Preuss, H (2004). *The Economics of Staging the Olympics; A Comparison of the Games 1972–2008.* Cheltenham, UK: Edward Elgar.

Price Waterhouse Coopers (2004). The economic impact of the Olympic Games. *European Economic Outlook,* June, 18–25.

Rahmann, B., & Kurscheidt, M (2002). The Soccer World Cup 2006 in Germany: choosing match locations by applying a modified cost–benefit model. In C. P. Barros, M. Ibrahímo, & S. Szymanski (Eds.), *Transatlantic Sport: The Comparative Economics of North American and European Sports*(pp. 171–203). Cheltenham, UK, and Northampton, MA: Edward Elgar.

Siegfried, J., & Zimbalist, A (2000). The economics of sports facilities and their communities. *The Journal of Economic Perspectives, 14,* 95–114.

Szymanski, S. (2002). The economic impact of World Cup 2002. *World Economics, 3*(1), 169–178.

Attracting Major Sporting Events: The Role of Local Residents

HOLGER PREUSS* & HARRY ARNE SOLBERG**

*Institute of Sport Science, Johannes Gutenberg-University, Germany **Trondheim Business School, Sør-Trøndelag University College, Norway

Different opinions exist regarding the economic value of hosting major sports events. Many consultancy reports conducted on behalf of event organizers predict positive impacts for the local economy and its residents—both in the short and long term. This, however, does not correspond with the opinion of many economists who have been sceptical and accused those producing the consultancy reports of exaggerating the benefits and under-estimating the costs (Crompton, 1995; Mules, 1998; Porter, 1999; Hultkrantz, 1998; Baade & Matheson, 2002, 2004; Preuss, 2004b; Késenne, 2005).

However, although the ability to create economic impacts has received substantial attention, it should be noted that achieving economic benefits was never the initial reason for staging mega sport events. Events such as the Olympics and international championships have a value of their own—first and foremost for competitors but increasingly, over the years, also for spectators. Local residents are provided with the opportunity to watch high-quality sporting competition and enjoy a festival atmosphere in their city. A successful event can also create "psychological income" such as a feeling of pride and unity among local residents and the national population (Howard & Crompton, 2005, p. 161). Hence, economic analyses alone cannot reflect the true social value of sports events.

Major sports events involve a number of stakeholders, among them are local residents. These stakeholders have different objectives for getting involved and some have conflicting interests. The latter aspect can apply to the distribution of revenues and costs between the local organizing committee and the international sports governing body that owns the event. History also reveals that those financing the event do not automatically expect to earn an equivalent proportion of the revenues.

Hosting mega-events requires substantial investment by the public sector in, for example, upgrading/improving the city's general infrastructure and sports facilities. Such investments need political decisions which allow a great number of individuals, organizations and private companies to benefit from them. For example, private entrepreneurs are hired to upgrade the local infrastructure and to construct new facilities, the tourism industry benefits from improved destination image and the host city benefits from additional national governmental subsidies. These examples illustrate the complexity of the impacts. Hosting events creates both winners and losers (Preuss, 2006), which explains why events seldom are embraced as "windows of opportunities" without opposition (Hiller, 1990, p. 120).

According to welfare economic theory, the public sector becomes involved in economic activities to prevent market failures. In this context, market failures occur if events that would have been beneficial are not hosted due to funding problems. In addition, the related welfare economic gains must exceed the gains from the alternative resource allocations.

The decision to stage a mega-event is the result of a political process involving local and national politicians as well as national and international sport governing bodies. In democracies, politicians need support from the populace. Therefore, this paper focuses on the role that local residents play in this process. After the literature review, the paper provides an overview of the various stakeholders who are directly and indirectly involved in the events. It also presents a theoretical model that helps to analyse the behaviour of these actors. The following section provides an overview of potential impacts from major sports events. On the basis of this, it discusses whether a rationale for public funding of events exists.

The empirical section presents the results from public opinion polls among local and national residents. This data come from 117 polls collected at 84 different locations. While the theoretical section explains the importance and role of local residents in the process of getting the public sector involved in attracting an event, this section analyses which (and how) factors influenced the residents' opinion. The final section discusses the lessons learned from these empirical analyses.

Literature Review

Literature concerning the role and importance of local residents when cities apply to host a major sport event is rare. However, the body of literature investigating impacts has grown considerably over the years. Many of these analyses pay special attention to economic impacts, covering both short- and long-term perspectives (Ritchie & Aitken, 1984; Hall, 1992; Kang & Perdue, 1994; Crompton, 1995; Hultkrantz, 1998; Mules, 1998; Spilling, 1998; Porter, 1999; Jones, 2001; Baade & Matheson, 2002, 2004; Solberg et al., 2002; Chalip, 2002; Chalip et al., 2003; Preuss, 2004a; Cashman, 2005; Késenne, 2005; Lee & Taylor, 2005; Oldenboom, 2006).

Several authors focus on the political importance of mega sport events, in particular the Olympic Games (Hill, 1996; Andranovich et al., 2001; Lenskyj, 2000, 2002). Other analyses investigate how and why local residents' opinion towards events is important for politicians in democracies. Hiller (1990) provides several common criticisms that prompt the need to assess residents' reactions and highlights the threat of increased taxes to pay for the event. Haxton (1999) investigates the perceived roles of community involvement in the mega-event hosting process. His study identifies discrepancies between the perceived roles and levels of host community involvement at different stages in the hosting process, from the viewpoint of the host public, community/welfare groups and organizers, and whether the level of perceived involvement influenced support for hosting Olympic Games.

A number of studies focus on residents' attitudes towards the Olympic Games. Ritchie & Lyons (1990) conducted several surveys in connection to the 1988 Calgary Winter Olympics. This work was later followed up by Mihailik (2001) in connection to the 1996 Summer Olympics in Atlanta. Miguélez & Carrasquer (1995) analysed the change in the labour market as a result of the 1992 Barcelona Olympics. Lenskyj (2002, pp. 151–182) discusses the public opinion on the Olympics in Sydney 2000 and De Lange (1998, p. 191) describes the public support for the Cape Town Olympic Bid for 2004. Finally, surveys on public opinion polls were conducted in connection to the 1994 Winter Olympics in Lillehammer (Spilling, 1994) and the 2006 Turin Winter Games (Scamuzzi, 2006).

Andersson et al. (2004) assess local residents' monetary valuation of hosting the 1997 World Skiing Championship by using the contingent valuation method, in terms of both willingness to pay (direct demand) and willingness to accept (compensated demand). Atkinson et al. (2006) use a similar approach when measuring the willingness to pay for hosting the 2012 London Olympics among residents in London, Manchester and Glasgow.

Theoretical Background on the Role and Importance of Local Residents in the Bidding Process for Mega Sport Events

An analysis of the role that local and national residents play in the bidding process for a mega sport event also requires an understanding of how the political system functions. Easton's (1965a) system analysis of a political system explains interactions between the various stakeholders involved in the process (Figure 1).

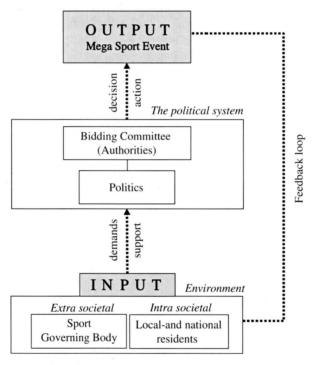

Figure 1. Simplified Dynamic Response Model of a Political System *Source*: Modified from Easton (1965a),p. 112)

In the centre we have the institutions of the political system, which are the "Bidding Committee" and the "Politicians". The environment can be split in two categories; the extra societal environment and the intra-societal environment. In this context, "local" and "national residents" represent the intra-societal environment, while the "sport governing body" represents the extra-societal environment. The environment concentrates its effects on two inputs: demand and support.

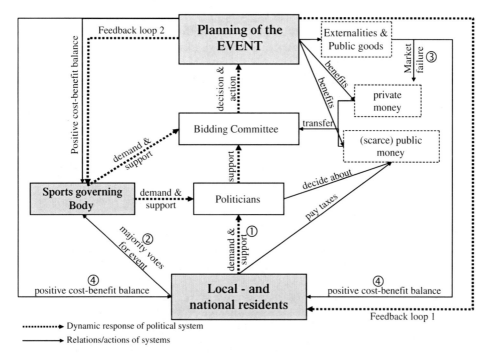

Figure 2. Model of Relations and Responses Based on Easton's System Analysis of Politics

Through them a vast range of changes in the environment may be channelled, reflected, and summarized. For this reason, they can be used as key indicators of how environmental events and conditions modify and affect the operations of the political system. (Easton, 1965a, p. 114)

Demand drives the motor of politics, and politics act on these intakes by converting demand into output through political authorities. The output is noticed by the environment through the feedback loop. If the residents' demand-stimulus leads to a satisfying response-outcome from the political institutions, they will continue supporting the political system, for example by paying taxes, conforming with laws and regulations, and also talk positively about political parties (Easton, 1965b, p. 159). However, Easton's input–throughput–output model has been criticized traditionally as failing to address what happens in the "black box", the core of the policy throughput process. Our use of the model here is reduced to the fact that politicians are turning environmental pressures or inputs from voters, into outputs. In reality this procedure is much more complex.

The model in Figure 1 can be implemented in a complex system where bidding for a major sport event is the issue (Figure 2). This converted model shows the main interrelations within the political system, and also how the extra and intra societal environment are involved in a bidding process. It visualises how the residents "desire" to host a sports event can be converted into demands in the political system (Easton, 1965a).

The residents (who are also voters) support politics as long as the outputs, which are the decisions and actions of the political system, "satisfy" their demand. In most democracies, politicians are elected for periods of three to five years. Following rational considerations (see Friedman & Hechter, 1988) politicians basically aim at being re-elected, which in turn influences their policy between elections (Downs, 1957).

Sport governing bodies (usually international sport federations) are autonomous extra-societal environments that want the residents and politicians to support the event for three reasons:

1. Politicians need the support of their constituents to be elected, which can work in their favour. To win bids, applicant cities (or nations) must convince the sport governing body that they can stage the event more successfully than their rivals. Due to this competition a successful event can be extremely expensive as it requires facilities as well as local infrastructure of high quality. Hence, it needs financial support from both the private and public sector. Politicians are more willing to fund event-related investments if local residents welcome the event.

2. Local residents create a positive atmosphere by attending the event as spectators which makes it a more enjoyable experience. The better the atmosphere the more welcome are the members of the sport governing body and politicians. All will feel good during the event and can use the opportunity to "bask in reflected glory" of the successfully staged event (Snyder *et al.*, 1986).

3. Events also serve to legitimate the continuing existence of sport governing bodies. The governing bodies support the political system by selecting host cities (nations) they believe can supply output—in this case an event—that is of sufficient quality (feedback loop). Successful events also tempt other cities to bid for future events. A fierce competition between many potential host cities provides the international sport governing body with bargaining power when negotiating with the local bidding commit-tee on how to distribute the event-related revenues and costs. It is well known that mega-events generate enormous revenues but also are highly expensive to host. The distribution of these revenues and costs depends on the level of competition at the demand and supply side. In recent years, many cities have bid for the Olympics and similar events. This situation has enabled international sport governing bodies to keep a large proportion of the revenues for themselves, while a high quality of sport arenas and other facilities is also required. Many cities were sceptical of hosting such events in the 1980s due to the negative financial results of the 1976 and 1972 Olympic Games in Montreal and Munich. As an illustration, the 1976 Winter Olympics was originally awarded to Denver, Colorado but was later moved to Innsbruck, Austria due to growing opposition among local residents in Colorado. Another example was when Los Angeles was the only candidate to host the 1984 Olympics. However, the bidding committee was private due to a public opinion poll which demanded not using public money for the Games. That put the

bidding committee under pressure to demand changes in the Olympic Charter. The fact that no other city was bidding forced the IOC into accepting many changes and allowed the organizing committee to commercialize the Games as well as keeping a greater proportion of revenues from sponsors and TV contracts for itself (Preuss, 2004a). As a consequence, the 1984 Los Angeles Games became very profitable for the organising committee.

With these three arguments in mind, it is surprising that the International Olympic Committee (IOC) weights "public opinion" as a sub-criterion out of 11 main topics by only 0.83% in regards to all criterion of the "Candidature Acceptance Procedure" which was adopted for the Olympic host city selection 2012 (IOC, 2006).

Impacts From Major Sporting Events

Figure 2 shows the interrelations between the different systems. To successfully bid for an event, the political system must agree to spend scarce public resources on it. Two sorts of rationale can justify this spending. One is the public "demand" (see arrow 4 in Figure 2), while the second is the risk for a market failure due to a free-rider mentality among those within the private sector who can benefit from the event (see arrow 3 in Figure 2). These aspects will be discussed in detail later.

Table 1 provides an overview of the main impacts from major sports events, and clearly illustrates the great complexity of these impacts.

Many of the impacts in Table 1 are public goods and externalities. Samuelson defines public goods as:

> ...goods which all enjoy in common in the sense that each individual's consumption of such a good leads to no subtractions from any other individual's consumption of that good. (Samuelson, 1954, p. 387)

This characteristic has become known as the non-rivalling criterion, meaning it is impossible for any individual to use up the good. Once a public good has been produced and offered to the customers, everybody can consume it free of charge—even simultaneously. In addition, pure public goods are also characterized by the non-excluding criterion. This means that it is impossible (or extremely expensive) to exclude any individual from consuming them—one example is public security (when one individual feels safe this does not prevent others from feeling safe). Impure public goods satisfy the non-rivalling criterion but not the non-excluding criterion. Visiting a sporting event in an indoor arena is an example of an impure public good as long as there are spare seats. The non-rivalling criterion is satisfied, while it is quite easy to prevent people from attending the event. Private goods, the opposite of public goods, do not possess any of these two properties. See Stiglitz (2000) for more details on the difference between private goods and public goods.

Table 1 Potential Impacts From Hosting Major Sports Events on Host Communities

Type of impact	Positive	Negative
Economic	• Increased economic activity • Creation of employment • Increase in labour supply • Increase in standard of living	• Price increase during event • Real estate speculation • Failure to attract tourists • Better alternative investments • Inadequate capital; and inadequate estimation of costs of event • Expensive security • Over indebtedness • Increased taxes
Tourism/ commercial	• Increased awareness of the region as a travel/tourism destination • Increased knowledge concerning the potential for investment and commercial activity in the region • Creation of new accommodation and tourist attractions; and	• Acquisition of poor reputation as a result of inadequate facilities, crime, improper practices or inflated prices • Negative reactions from existing enterprises due to the possibility of new competition for local manpower and government assistance
Physical/ environmental	• Construction of new facilities • Improvement of local infrastructure • Preservation of heritage • Environmental promotion • Impacts on sport	• Ecological damage • Changes in natural processes • Architectural pollution • Destruction of heritage • Overcrowding • Unused facilities
Social/cultural	• Increase in permanent level of local interest and participation in types of activity associated with event • Strengthening of regional values and traditions	• Commercialization of activities which may be of a personal or private nature • Modification of nature of event or activity to accommodate tourism • Potential increase in crime • Changes in community structure • Social dislocation
Psychological	• Increased local pride and community spirit • Increased awareness of non-local perceptions • Festival atmosphere during event	• Tendency toward defensive attitudes concerning host region • Culture shock • Misunderstandings leading to varying degrees of host/visitor hostility

Table 1 (*Continued*)

Type of impact	Positive	Negative
Political/ administrative	• Enhanced international recognition of region and values • Development of skills among planners • International understanding	• Economic exploitation of local population to satisfy ambitions of political elite • Distortion of true nature of event to reflect elite values • Failure to cope • Inability to achieve aims • Increase in administrative costs • Use of event to legitimate unpopular decisions • Legitimating of ideology and sociocultural reality • Corruption

Sources: Hall (1992); Voeth & Liehr (2003); Scamuzzi (2006); Hiller (1990); Preuss (1998); Cashman (2005)

Externalities refer to the impact on others as a result of an activity that causes incidental benefits or damages with no corresponding compensation provided or paid by those who generate them. Hence, neither the costs nor the benefits will be included in the market price. Noise from a stadium is an example of a negative externality, while improved estate value from the upgrading of an area around a stadium is an example of a positive externality.

Most externalities can also be regarded as public goods. Upgrading an area around a stadium improves the view for all neighbours. Those living in the area do not reduce the ability for one another to enjoy the improved view. Furthermore, it is impossible to exclude the neighbourhood from enjoying the view unless you put up a fence around the upgraded area. There can also be negative externalities that have public goods characteristics. Too many crowds in the city during an event are examples of negative public goods that have both the non-excluding and non-rivalling characteristics.

Many of the impacts in Table 1 both satisfy the criteria of public goods and externalities. As an example, increased attention of the host destination is an externality since it mainly will benefit the local tourism industry, not the event organizing committee. In principle, this will benefit all firms within the tourism industry, not only one hotel. Hence, it can be regarded both as a public good and an externality (see Figure 2).

If the event creates a festival atmosphere within the city, it will be impossible to exclude local residents and visitors from enjoying it. Furthermore, that one person enjoys it, does not reduce the ability of others to do the same. Indeed, it is the joint participation in the event and city life from many people that creates the festival atmosphere. Hence, peoples' involvement in the event can be regarded as an input in the production of the atmosphere. Another example is that the construction of new and better sports facilities for the event can motivate more local residents to practice sport after the event is over. It is well documented that sporting activities improve people's health conditions or at least participation in sports (Gratton & Taylor, 2000). This in turn can reduce absenteeism from work so that the production (and consumption) of goods and services in society increases. Hence, such impacts are examples of externalities. Price increases of other goods and services, in the literature known as pecuniary externalities, or corruption are examples of negative public goods which are also displayed in Table 1.

Hosting mega sport events can be extremely expensive, but this is not in itself a rationale for publicly funding them. On the other hand, the existence of public goods and externalities leading to market failure can represent such a rationale. The reason for this is that free-rider motives among the beneficiaries of the impacts can prevent events that are a socioeconomic benefit for the destination (nation) as a unit from being hosted. The risk of free-riding behaviour is rooted in the non-excluding criteria that characterises many of the potential impacts that are created by the event. This is a well known phenomenon in the welfare economic literature (Olson, 1971). According to welfare economic theory, governments should only be involved in hosting events in order to prevent the market failure of attracting an event if the value of the aggregated benefits would exceed the value of the costs and also that it exceed the gains from the alternative resource allocations.

The local tourism industry profits will increase with additional tourists. Private companies will benefit from improvements in public transportation, new roads, highways or airports, and also from higher security level that can last for years. An upgrading of the city's infrastructure and new sports facilities can make the city more attractive as a place in which to locate businesses. This can create jobs and income for local companies, local residents and the local public sector. As already mentioned, new sport facilities can stimulate improvement in people's health, which in turn can increase society's productivity.

Nevertheless, those who reap the economic fruits from these (and other) event-related benefits will maximize their benefits (profit and/or utility) from adopting a free-rider strategy. If so, the result can be that the city (nation) as a unit spends a sub-optimal level of resources—also during the application process for the event. The fierce competition among bid cities reduces the chances for sub-optimally planned events to be elected as host (see feedback loop 2 in Figure 2; Preuss, 2004b). To win the bid, the city (nation) must convince the sport governing body of its attractiveness and also that its infrastructure and facilities will be of a high standard.

The localization of a sports event is not distributed by market mechanism but is the result of political processes. The initiative to bid for events usually comes from private groups or local politicians. Their intentions can be different from those of the residents (Preuss, 2006). For example, the initiative to bid for the Olympics in Atlanta 1996 came from the private construction industry seeking new contracts. Another example is that the

Barcelona local politicians wanted the Games to redevelop the city, the Catalan government wanted to promote Catalonia as a rival to Madrid, and the central government wanted to control the Games as Spanish Games (Botella, 1995, p. 143). These objectives were used to justify the substantial public investment during the Olympiad and to create within the city and the province of Catalonia the desired impetus to make good the long term under-investment in leisure, culture, sport and transportation during previous decades (Millet, 1995, 191).

Residents will base their opinions on the expected impacts from the events. In a rational world, they will make up their mind on the basis of individual cost–benefit considerations. If they expect the costs to exceed the perceived benefits, then following Homans' (1961), pp. 317–318) exchange theory, they will vote against it. In practice, however, Simon's (1982) theory on bounded rationality is relevant to describe the residents' behaviour. Residents will base their opinion about the event on sources such as:

- Information from the bidding committee, local politicians, the media and lobby groups—also including people opposing the events.
- Information from previous host cities, for example through the media.
- Personal experiences from other sport events, inside or outside the destination.

(Preuss, 2004a, p. 49)

However, most people will not have a complete overview of all the event-related impacts, neither for themselves nor for the destination (nation). Therefore, they will not know the real cost–benefit balance of a future mega sport event in their own city.

Facing demand from the residents (in the political system), the politicians may be willing to fund the infrastructure necessary for the event. This, in turn, can prevent market failures given that the aggregated benefits from the event exceed the costs of staging it. Those who want the city/nation to apply for the event will channel their demand towards the "political system". Figure 2 illustrates how the residents' opinion can influence the chance of being awarded the event. The fact that residents play a role in the process makes it important for the political system to uphold the demand, once the decision to support it has been taken. A massive support from the residents will make it easier to grant public funding.

Public opinion polls are often used to measure whether residents support hosting an event. The empirical section in this paper shows that approximately 76% of the residents felt a positive cost–benefit balance and therefore would have voted in favour of hosting. This "want" to host events can be translated into "demand" directed as "input" towards the "political system".

The next section will present the results from opinion polls among residents, covering both locals and the rest of the nation. The data come from both previous and future host cities (nations), as well as applicants for future events.

Data Set and Methodology

In this section we analyse the secondary data from 117 opinion polls that were collected at 84 different locations (cities and nations) representing 54 events. The variable poll describes the average support of residents in favour of hosting an event. In cases of more than one poll from one period, we used the arithmetic mean from all these polls, both in the descriptive analyses and the regression analyses.

The data for the independent variables come from the CIA World Fact books (www.cia.gov) 2006 (www.theodora.com/wfb/abc_world_fact_-book.html) and OECD's Factbook from 2006 (www.oecd.org/dataoecd/32/21/36029941.html). The distribution of events was as follows:

- Olympic Games (n =45)
- EURO (football) (n =6)
- Rugby World Championship (n =1)
- World Championship skiing, Nordic Games (n =1)
- FIFA football World Cup finals (n =1).

The polls were conducted between 1990 and 2006, with the exception of those in connection with the 1988 Calgary Winter Olympics. The sample includes both events that have been hosted as well as future events, as illustrated by the distribution below:

- Events already hosted (n =12)
- Cities (nations) that lost the bid competition (n =34)
- Cities that have won bids—but where the event has not yet been hosted (n =3)
- Applicant for future events where a decision not has been made (n =5).

The first section of the data analyses present descriptive statistics, while the second presents the results form Ordinary Least "Square" regressions. Here, POLL was the dependent variable, while we had a set a potentially seven independent variables (see Table 5). This included two dummy variables; POLSYS (the political system) and EVEXP (event experience). Both dummies may have an influence on the opinion polls (POLL), but do not depend on the other predictors.

Results and Discussions

The support from the residents has a different importance in the process of bidding and preparing a major sporting event. Therefore, we checked if the opinion polls changed over time. The data were grouped in the following four periods:

1. The "pre-bid period" (21 polls) covers the period before an official bid campaign starts. In this period, the first media announcements of a potential bid are launched and results of feasibility studies are presented. For the Olympic Games this period covers all public opinion polls nine to

12 years before the Games. During this period politicians are open to look at the population's opinion, which so far is not influenced by campaigns.

2. "Bid" is the period after the declaration of intent of the city towards the sport governing body to bid for an event (n =52). For Olympic Games this period covers a little more than two years and is split into an "applicant city" phase and a "candidate city" phase. During this period the bidding committee runs campaigns to market the idea of staging the event. Politicians often back the bidding committee, especially when public resources are used to run the bidding campaign, which can be several million euros in the case of the Olympics.

3. "Preparation" is the period which starts right after winning the bid and ends on the eve of the event (n =37). For Olympic Games this covers seven years. During this period public opinion is not as important to the organizing committee as it is to the politicians. Each democratic nation has an election during the period of preparation. Campaigns are launched to keep positive opinion towards the event high, in order to avoid negative public opinions caused by the intensive spending of public resources and the occurence of (small and large) scandals.

4. "Post-event" is the period that covers all data from polls after the event (n =7). During this period the population has memories of the event.

The mean value in Table 2 displays the proportion that was in favour of hosting the particular event during the four periods. Although the mean opinion varies across the periods, there are no statistical differences between the periods at a 5% level.

Table 3 displays the differences in mean values between different categories of events and also between groups. The data in Table 3 revealed some differences, but these differences were not statistically significant according to *t*-tests. It is worth noting that there was no difference in opinions between local residents and "the rest of the nation"—either for one-city events, or for events that were hosted in several cities. Another result was that people living in cities that had previously hosted such events were not more positive than those living in cities without such an experience.

Table 2 Percentage of Residents in Favour of Hosting the Event by Period

Period	N*	N**	N***	Min.	Max.	Mean	Std deviation
Pre-bid period	21	14	–	39.0**	88.5**	69.7**	15.75**
Bid period	52	39	–	32.0**	96.2**	77.6**	14.49**
Preparation period	37	10	–	53.0**	96.0**	82.4**	12.41**
Post-event period	7	5	–	47.0**	95.0**	77.2**	18.09**
Average all periods	117		54	32.0***	96.0***	75.7***	15.36***

Notes:
* Number of opinion polls.
** Number of average polls per period per event.
*** Number of average polls per event.

Table 3 Statistics of Differences by Location Asked, Bids Won and Type of Event and Event Experience

| | N | Local residents/population in favour of an event% | | |
		mean	Std deviation	t-value (sig.)
All events				
Local residents	47	77.27	14.90	0.004 (ns)
National population	31	77.28	12.50	
One-city event				
Local residents	45	76.84	15.07	0.120 (ns)
National population	23	77.27	12.14	
Event hosted in several cities				
Local residents	2	87.00	4.24	0.907 (ns)
National population	8	77.31	14.35	
Winning the bid				
Won a bid	24	79.34	12.61	0.83 (ns)
Lost a bid	48	76.46	14.41	
Experience with mega-events				
No experience	39	77.73	15.74	0.345 (ns)
Previous host	38	76.63	12.10	

The same pattern of no significant difference applied to cities that had been awarded events and cities that failed to win the bid competition. Note that in Table 3, N refers to the number of polls, which is different from the other tables where N refers to the number of events.

The econometric analysis tested seven potential explanatory variables. These were selected via correlation analysis from originally 15 potential influencing variables we identified. The lack of statistical significant differences displayed in Table 3 gave us reason for rejecting several potential dummy variables, such as distinguishing between locals and nationals, winning a bid or not, events in one or several cities. The selection of variables used for the regression was based on the findings in Table 4. It presents the correlation between the dependent variable POLL and the predictors we expected could influence peoples' opinion towards the events. That we not had access to individual data files reduced the ability to select other explanatory variables.

The fact that Table 2 only revealed a few significant differences between the periods allowed us to use arithmetic means without weighting any of them when constructing the regression analysis. Hence, the dependent variable POLL describes the average percentage in favour of the event of all polls executed.

Table 4 Correlations Between Support Proportion and Potential Independent Variables

	Average support (POLL)	Sig. (2-tailed)	N
GDPCAP	−.443(**)	.001	53
PUBDEBT	−.369(*)	.032	34
GROWTH	.357(*)	.010	51
GINI	.338(*)	.014	52
UNEMPL	.228	.100	53

Notes:
** Correlation (Pearson) is significant at the 0.01 level (2-tailed).
* Correlation (Pearson) is significant at the 0.05 level (2-tailed).

Results of the Regression Analysis and Discussions

The regression analysis included all the potential independent variables displayed in Table 5.

$$POLL = \beta_0 + \beta_1 GDPCAP + \beta_2 PUBDEBT + \beta_3 GROWTH + \beta_4 GINI$$
$$+ \beta_5 UNEMPL + \beta_6 POLSYS + \beta_7 EVEXP + \varepsilon$$

Several alternatives were tested in order to find the best-fitting model—experimenting both with the number of variables and function forms. The restricted number of data, 34 (OECD members) and 54 (all countries), reduced the number of explanatory variables in the regression. The following equation turned out as the best alternative.

$$POLL = \beta_0 + \beta_1 GDPCAP^2 + \beta_2 PUBDEBT + \beta_3 PUBDEBT^3$$
$$+ \beta_4 GROWTH + \varepsilon$$

The Durbin–Watson variable (1.889) indicates no autocorrelation, while the VIF-indexes indicate that multicollinearity did not occur. Furthermore the Cook–Weisenberg test was insignificant (chi^2 =0.37, p >0.05), which indicated no heteroskedasticity in the sample. In addition, its results correspond with our expectations based on economic theory.

GDP per capita (GDPCAP) had a negative effect on residents' "want" to host major events. This does not correspond with the idea of sport as a luxury good. An explanation is that major sports events should not be regarded as a typical sports product. A reasonable explanation for this can be that people are aware that the hosting of such events can be extremely expensive. This can reduce the production of other goods and services in society—particularly if they are funded by the public sector. Those who oppose the events often use such arguments in discussions about the events' socioeconomic value. On the other hand, the events can also produce a legacy, for example by upgrading the local infrastructure, also including new sport facilities.

Expectations that the events will influence other goods and services within the host destination (nation) makes it difficult to separate the "event-consumption effect" (sport as a luxury good) in demand analyses. For

Table 5 Overview and Description of Potential Explanatory Variable

GDPCAP =Gross domestic product per capita adjusted by the purchasing power parities during the year of the poll. This measure is sufficient to compare welfare and living conditions across countries. Sport is often assumed to be a luxury good, and this and the former variable will indicate whether this applies to sport event.

PUBDEBT =Public sector debt as percentage of GDP per capita. The data are the average public sector (national government) deficit from the three years before the poll was conducted. A negative sign means a deficit, while a positive sign means a surplus. The hypothesis is that the higher the public debts of a state the less people want an event, because they are aware that no public resources can be additionally spent for a mega-event and there is a general fear of over-indebtedness of the state (Preuss, 1998). However, such concerns are more likely in less-populated nations, than in heavy populated nations, e.g. in China and the US, where the costs of hosting a mega-event will be a drop in the ocean on a macroeconomic level. We therefore calculated the variable in per-capita term.

GROWTH =Percentage growth in GDP. The hypothesis is that countries which have a high growth of their GDP do support the idea to host a mega sport event more than those with low growth.

GINI =Gini-coefficient. This coefficient is a measure of inequality of income in a country. The coefficient is between 0 and 1, where 0 corresponds to perfect equality of income. The hypothesis is, that the higher the coefficient, the more people want an event, because the poor expect employment and general economic activity and the rich entertainment and a gentrified urban development.

UNEMPL =Unemployment rate. The hypothesis is that the higher the unemployment rate the more people are in favour to stage a mega sport event, because they hope that jobs will be created through the event.

POLSYS. This is a dummy variable that distinguishes between former Western countries and former Eastern bloc countries (plus communism systems, here Cuba and China). The reasoning in our model assumes that nations with a long tradition in democracy—where politicians aim at being re-elected—motivates politicians to adopt a strategy that can make them popular among the residents (voters)—for example by applying for popular sports events. We wanted to test whether any differences between democracies and former and actual dictatorships could be found.

EVEXP =Experience with hosting major sporting events. This is a dummy variable that distinguishes between locations that have hosted major sports events in the past 30 years before the bid and those that have not hosted them. One reason for this could be that people with positive experiences from previous events—and therefore would be more positive towards hosting them again (see Homans' stimulus proposition 1961). A negative result would indicate the opposite—that people were dissatisfied with the event and its impacts.

example, when London hosts the 2012 Olympics, people outside the UK will not worry whether it influences the production of other goods and services within London or the UK. They only see the consumption of the sport event. This is different for Londoners who may worry about negative legacy on production or have hopes of a positive long-term legacy. Hence, people's opinions towards such events are not only a matter of consumption but also of production.

Another reason for the negative sign on the GDP-coefficient can be that countries with low per capita income hope the event will stimulate economic activity, and hence increase their own income. However, here it is worth bearing in mind that many economists have serious doubts whether major events really have such effects. Hence, such hopes may well be based on unrealistic expectations.

A third—and different—explanation can be that low-income groups consider the events as a joyful escape from a problematic life. However, we do not have any data that enable us to test this and similar hypotheses. Therefore, further discussions on this topic will be speculative—but nevertheless an interesting topic for future research.

We used GDPCAP as a squared value, because that increases the values of rich nations more and fits better in describing the opinion polls.

Our model reveals that high per capita public debt (PUBDEBT) increased scepticism towards the events. The higher the per capita public deficit during the three years before the poll, the less supportive people were. Such attitudes correspond with previous research which has documented that people fear that mega-events can lead to over-indebtedness (Preuss, 1998).

Nonlinear tests of this variable showed that a function of power three best expressed the relationship between the dependent variable (POLL) and "the public debt variable" (PUBDEBT). Arguments for using a variable twice in the same regression model are given in Frick (2001). The equation and signs on the coefficients revealed most scepticism towards the events in low-populated nations with high public sector deficit. People in heavy populated nations, such as the USA and China, will know that the event related costs are only a "drop in the ocean" on a macroeconomic level. Unfortunately, we only had data from 34 nations (OECD members) on this variable.

As expected, economic growth (GROWTH) had a positive effect on people's desire to host the events. The population is used to changes in their environment and values the positive economic changes coming along with growth. Major events are perceived as a catalyst to develop. We do not regard this result as a contradiction with the negative sign on the GDP-

Model 1:

	B	Std error	t	Sig.	Collinearity (tolerance)	Collinearity (VIF)
(Constant)	83.03	3.72	22.33	.000		
GDPCAP^2	−.030	.01	−4.00	.000	.649	1.541
PUBDEBT	4.17	9.69	4.30	.000	.167	5.077
PUBDEBT^3	−1.17	2.35	−7.864	.000	.208	4.809
GROWTH	3.44	.73	6.635	.000	.841	1.190

Notes:
Dependent variable: POLL
Durbin–Watson: 1.842
Std error of the estimate: 9.706
Adjusted R square: 0.600

coefficient. While GDP is an indication of the nation's wealth, the growth variable only indicates whether the economic development was positive or negative when the polls were conducted. Many examples illustrate that nations with low per capita income, nevertheless, can have high economic growth and vice versa.

In addition, we also tested a large number of alternative regressions, altering the seven variables explained in Table 5 as well as the functions. Some tests indicated that the income distribution (Gini-coefficient) had some effect on the dependent variable, with people in nations with unequal income distribution (low coefficient) being the most positive towards staging an event. One reason for this can be that many impacts (see Table 1) have characteristics of public goods and externalities. This means that everybody is able to benefit from them free of charge. As an example, if the event leaves behind improved local transportation, everybody within the region can benefit from it. However, we do not emphasize this result as much for the other variables in our model, which has a higher adjusted r^2.

The variable UNEMPL (unemployment rate) did not show any significant results in any of our models. The two dummy variables (POLSYS and EVEXP) which filter the group by their political system and previous event experience did not show any significant influences. For EVEXP, this confirmed the results that were uncovered by the t-test (see Table 3).

Concluding Remarks

Many groups with different objectives are directly or indirectly involved in the bidding of major sports event. Local and national residents play an important role in this process, although the decisions to apply and host the event are in the hands of other groups. International sport governing bodies select the hosts—but want support from residents as well as politicians. To be elected as a host, applicant cities and nations must convince them that they are able to produce high-quality events. This can make the events extremely expensive, and therefore the bidding and later organizing committees need financial funding from the public sector.

Many impacts from a major sport event (see Table 1) have characteristics of public goods and externalities. This can represent a potential rationale for public funding of events according to welfare economic theory. Without public funding, a free-rider mentality among the potential beneficiaries (especially private industry) can prevent events that would have been beneficial for the destination as a unit from being hosted. Politicians, however, need backing from voters and will find it easier to support events that are popular among the residents.

In regards to the question of what influences the positive opinions on hosting a major sport event we analysed data from 117 opinion polls collected in connection to 54 events. The analysis revealed that approximately three of four were positive towards hosting major sports events. Surprisingly, support was strongest in low-income nations. This indicates that the hosting of a major sporting event cannot be regarded as a luxury good, which is a common assumption for sports goods. People are aware the events can influence the production of other goods and services in society. Hence, their opinions are not only a matter of consumption, but also of production. This reasoning was supported by the tendency of extra scepticism in nations with high public sector debt. The regression analysis revealed that economic growth had a positive influence towards the events.

References

Andranovich, G. D., Burbank, M. J., & Heying, Ch. H. (2001). Olympic cities: lessons learned from mega-event politics. *Journal of Urban Affairs, 23*(2), 113–131.

Andersson, T. D., Rustad, A., & Solberg, H. A. (2004). Local residents' monetary evaluation of sports events. *Managing Leisure, 9*(3), 145–158.

Atkinson, G., Mourato, S., & Szymanski, S. (2006). *Are we Willing to Pay Enough to "Back the Bid"? Valuing the Intangible Impacts of Hosting the Summer Olympic Games.* Memo, London School of Economics.

Baade, R., & Matheson, V. (2002). Upon further review: an examination of sporting event economic impact studies. *The Sport Journal, 5*(1). Retrieved 27.02.2006 from: www.thesportjournal.org/2002Journal/Vol5-No1/studies.htm

Baade, R., & Matheson, V. (2004). The quest for the cup: assessing the economic impact of the World Cup. *Regional Science, 38*(4), 341–352.

Botella, J. (1995). The political games: agents and strategies in the 1992 Barcelona Olympic Games. In M. Moragas Spá, & M. Botella (Eds.), *The Keys to Success*(pp. 139–148). Barcelona: Centre d'Estudis Olímpics i de l'Esport.

Cashman, R. (2005). *The Bitter-Sweet Awakening. The Legacy of the Sydney 2000 Olympic Games.* Sydney: Walla Walla Press.

Chalip, L. (2002). *Using the Olympics to Optimise Tourism Benefits.* Retrieved 2 January, 2006 from http://olympicstudies.uab.es/lectures/web/abs.asp?id_llico =7

Chalip, L., Green, B. C., & Hill, B. (2003). Effects of sport event media on destination image and intention to visit. *Journal of Sport Management, 17*(3), 214–234.

Crompton, J. L. (1995). Economic impact analysis of sports facilities and events: eleven sources of misapplication. *Journal of Sport Management, 9*(1), 14–35.

De Lange, P. (1998). *The Games Cities Play.* Pretoria: C.P. de Lange Inc.

Downs, A. (1957). *An Economic Theory of Democracy.* New York: Harper.

Easton, D. (1965a). *A Framework for Political Analysis.* Engelwood Cliffs, NJ: Prentice Hall.

Easton, D. (1965b). *A System Analysis of Political Life.* New York, NY: Wiley and Sons.

Frick, B. (2001). Die Einkommen von Superstars und Wasserträgern im professionellen Teamsport. *Zeitschrift für Betriebswirtschaftslehre, 71*(6), 702–721.

Friedman, D., & Hechter, M. (1988). The contribution of rational choice theory to macrosociological research. *Sociological Theory, 6*(2), 201–218.

Gratton, C., & Taylor, P. (2000). *Economics of Sport and Recreation.* London: Roudledge.

Hall, C. M. (1992). *Hallmark Tourist Events—Impacts, Management & Planning.* London: Bellhaven Press.

Haxton, P. (1999). *Community Participation in the Mega-Event Hosting Process: the Case of the Olympic Games.* PhD thesis, University of Technology, Sydney (UTS).

Hill, C. R. (1996). *Olympic Politics. Athens to Atlanta 1896–1996.* Manchester: Manchester University Press.

Hiller, H. H. (1990). *The urban transformation of a landmark event: The 1988 Calgary Winter Olympics Urban Affairs Quarterly, 26*(1), 118–137.

Homans, G. C. (1961). *Social Behaviour. Its Elementary Forms.* London: Routledge & Kegan Paul.

Howard, D. R., & Crompton, J. L. (2005). *Financing Sport* (2nd edn). Morgantown: Fitness Information Technology.

Hultkrantz, L. (1998). Mega-event displacement of visitors: the World Championship in Athletics, Göteborg 1995. *Festival Management & Event Tourism*, 5(1), 1–8.

IOC (2006). *Candidature Acceptance Procedure. XXII Olympic Winter Games in 2012*. Lausanne: IOC.

Jones, C. (2001). Mega-events and host-region impacts: determining the true worth of the 1999 Rugby World Cup. *International Journal of Tourism Research*, 3(3), 241–251.

Kang, Y. S., & Perdue, R. (1994). Long-term impact of a mega-event on international tourism to the host country: a conceptual model and the case of the 1988 Seoul Olympics. *Journal of International Consumer Marketing*, 6, 205–225.

Kèsenne, S. (2005). Do we need an economic impact study or a cost–benefit analysis of a sport event? *European Sport Management Quarterly*, 5(2), 133–142.

Lee, C.-K., & Taylor, T. (2005). Critical reflections on the economic impact assessment of a mega-event: the case of 2002 FIFA World Cup. *Tourism Management*, 26(4), 595–603.

Lenskyj, H. J. (2000). *Inside the Olympic Industry: Power, Politics and Activism*. New York: State University of New York.

Lenskyj, H. J. (2002). *The Best Olympics Ever? Social Impacts of Sydney 2000*. Albany, NY: State University of New York Press.

Miguélez, F., & Carrasquer, P. (1995). The reprecussion of the Olympic Games labour. In M. Moragas, & M. Botella (Eds.), *The Keys to Success*(pp. 149–164). Barcelona: Centre d'Estudis Olímpics i de l'Esport.

Mihalik, B. (2001). Host population perceptions of the 1996 Atlanta Olympics: attendance, support, benefits and liabilities. *Tourism Analysis*, 5(1), 49–53.

Millet, L. (1995). The games of the city. In M. Moragas, & M. Botella (Eds.), *The Keys to Success*(pp. 188–202). Barcelona: Centre d'Estudis Olímpics i de l'Esport.

Mules, T. (1998). Taxpayer subsidies for major sporting events. *Sport Management Review*, 1(1), 25–43.

Oldenboom, E. R. (2006). *Costs and Benefits of Major Sports Events: A Case Study of Euro 2000*. Amsterdam: Meerwaade.

Olson, M. (1971). *The Logic of Collective Action. Public Goods and the Theory of Groups*. Cambridge, MA: Harvard University Press.

Porter, P. (1999). Mega-sports events as municipal investments: a critique of impact analysis. In J. L. Fizel, E. Gustafson, & L. Hadley (Eds.), *Sports Economics: Current Research*. New York: Praeger Press.

Preuss, H. (1998). Problemizing arguments of the opponents of Olympic Games. In R. K. Barney, K. B. Wamsley, S. G. Martyn, & G. H. MacDonald (Eds.), *Global and Cultural Critique: Problematising the Olympic Games* (pp. 197–218), Fourth International Symposium for Olympic Research. London: ON.

Preuss, H. (2004a). *The Economics of Staging the Olympics. A Comparison of the Games 1972–2008*. Cheltenham, UK: Edward Elgar.

Preuss, H. (2004b). Olympische Spiele 2012 in Deutschland. Der stärkste Bewerbungswettbewerb in der olympischen Geschichte. In H.-D. Horch, J. Heydel, & A. Sierau (Eds.), *Events im Sport. Marketing, Management, Finanzierung*(pp. 225–238). Köln: Deutsche Sporthochschule Koeln.

Preuss, H. (2006). The Olympic Games: winners and losers. In B. Houlihan (Ed.), *Sport and Society* (2nd edn). London, Thousand Oaks, CA, New Delhi: Sage.

Ritchie, J. R., & Aitken, K. (1984). Assessing the impacts of the 1988 Olympic Winter Games: the research programme and initial results. *Journal of Travel Research*, 22(3), 17–25.

Ritchie, J. R. B., & Lyons, M. (1990). Olympulse VI: a post-event assessment of resident reaction to the XV Olympic Winter Games. *Journal of Travel Research*, 23(3), 14–23.

Samuelson, P. A. (1954). The pure theory of public expenditure. *Review of Economics and Statistics*, 36(4), 387–389.

Scamuzzi, S. (2006). Winter Olympic Games 2006 in Turin: the rising weight of public opinion. In N. Müller, M. Messing, & H. Preuß (Eds.),. *From Chamonix to Turin. The Winter Games in the Scope of Olympic Research* (pp. 343–357). Olympische Studien, Vol. 8. Kassel: Agon.

Simon, H. A. (1982). *Models of Bounded Rationality*. Cambridge, MA: MIT Press.

Snyder, C. R., Lassegard, M. A., & Ford, C. E. (1986). Distancing after group success and failure: basking in reflected glory and cutting off reflected failure. *Journal of Personality and Social Psychology*, *51*(2), 382–388.

Solberg, H. A., Andersson, T. D., & Shibli, S. (2002). An exploration of the direct economic impacts from business travellers at world championships. *Event Management*, *7*(3), 151–164.

Spilling, O. (1994). *OL's Næringsmessige betydning på kort og lang sikt*. Sluttrapport fra prosjektet 'Regionale virkninger av OL'. Lillehammer. Østlandsforskning, Rapport nr. 26–1994.

Spilling, O. (1998). Beyond intermezzo. On the long-term industrial impacts of mega-events. The case of Lillehammer 1994. *Festival Management & Event Tourism*, *5*(3), 101–122.

Stiglitz, J. E. (2000). *Economics of the Public Sector* (3rd Edn). New York: Norton.

Voeth, M. & Liehr, M. (2003). *Akzeptanz und Einstellungen der Bevölkerung gegenüber dem Sportgroßereignis „FIFA WM 2006". Die Situation 2003*. Hohenheimer Arbeits- und Projektberichte zum Marketing, No. 8.

Index